TWENTIETH CENTURY INTERPRETATIONS
OF

GRAY'S
ELEGY

A Collection of Critical Essays

Edited by
HERBERT W. STARR

Prentice-Hall, Inc. *Englewood Cliffs, N. J.*

A SPECTRUM BOOK

Acknowledgments

I am particularly grateful to my wife, who has helped me with much of the routine work, and to Professor Ian Jack, who very kindly and carefully condensed his original article to a length more suitable for this book. I have also received assistance from George W. Kreuzberger, J. Raymond Hendrickson, John P. Eden, Jr., Carl Anderson, William Powell Jones, John Sutherland, and the staff of Haverford Library.

Contents

PART FOUR—*View Points*

Introduction

by Herbert W. Starr

Thomas Gray (1716–1771) was the son of Philip Gray, a scrivener and exchange broker, and Dorothy Antrobus, who with her sister Mary conducted a millinery business. The couple was moderately prosperous financially, but of their twelve children only Thomas survived childhood. Thomas's early years could not have been very happy ones, for his father was a penurious, jealous, bad-tempered man, who occasionally beat his wife. Very probably it was this atmosphere which prompted Dorothy, an affectionate and conscientious parent, to agree with her brothers, Robert and William, who were masters at Eton, that her son should be sent to that school when he was only eight years old.

Eton in the eighteenth century was by no means like the Eton of the twentieth century. Little training was given save in the classics while most of the students were rowdy and undisciplined. A reserved and studious boy like Gray would not have found school life very pleasant. Naturally he formed a friendship with three other rather quiet boys. Half-humorously, half-romantically, they called themselves the "Quadruple Alliance" and provided each other with names culled from classical or melodramatic literature: Gray was known as Orosmades, Thomas Ashton as Almanzor, Richard West, a talented and poetic youth, as Favonius or Zephyrille, and Horace Walpole, the son of Sir Robert Walpole, the most powerful politician in England, as Celadon. All wrote Latin verse, largely as class assignments, but both Gray and West became gifted Anglo-Latin poets. Although the four friends carried on a lively correspondence, the Alliance was somewhat disrupted when Walpole, Gray, and Ashton went to Cambridge University and West to Oxford.

At Cambridge's Peterhouse College Gray was supported partly by a scholarship and partly by the earnings of his mother's shop, for his father had always refused to contribute any money to his education. Though he disliked the prospect, he was expected to study law, which in that era was about as close to business training as the universities could provide. Gray did not find life at Cambridge particularly stimulating, since in the eighteenth century both the students and faculties of the two great English universities were at a rather low ebb intellectually. But in other respects his situation soon improved. In 1735 his mother, finding her husband's behavior even more intolerable than usual, threatened to leave him. This seems to have had a somewhat restraining effect on Philip, for that gallant gentleman valued the income from the shop which Dorothy and her sister operated. About the same time, Thomas's aunt, Sarah Gray died; and, as the principal beneficiary of her will, he came into a small income.

In 1739 Horace Walpole was to take the "Grand Tour"—that is, he was to make that leisurely trip across the Continent which was regarded as the culmination of a fashionable and wealthy young gentleman's education, since it supposedly acquainted him with the finest cultural achievements of continental Europe. Unfortunately, the young gentleman making the Tour often paid little attention to Continental culture, acquiring instead a well-rounded education in Continental vices. Sir Robert Walpole suffered from no delusions concerning the innate virtue of man. The ideal companion for his mercurial son, he felt, was a studious, reliable, and highly respectable youth such as Thomas Gray. Consequently, he offered to pay all Gray's expenses if he would accompany Horace, and for the next two years the young men traveled through France, Switzerland, and Italy. This was an influential period in Gray's life: the poverty of the European lower classes, Racine and the French drama, the superb scenery of the Alps (in his enthusiasm for the latter he clearly foreshadowed the nineteenth-century Romantics), Italian art and literature—all this and a great deal more that he saw interested him enormously.

Despite a promising beginning, however, all did not go well between Walpole and Gray. By the spring of 1741 relations between them had become strained. Actually the two, though friends, were not sufficiently congenial to withstand so long a period together: both were young, inexperienced, rather sensitive, and proud. Gray, although he had social capabilities and a highly developed sense of humor, had matured intellectually much more rapidly than Walpole. He had become a devoted scholar, far more interested in architecture, art galleries, and libraries than in dances. In scholarly matters, Walpole, though clever, was a dilettante. He was witty, lively, frivolous at times, extremely social, and polished. Moreover, he was too aware (as was Gray himself in a different sense) of his friend's financial dependence on him and of his own position as the wealthy and popular son of England's prime minister. The immediate reason for their quarrel is not known, although malicious meddling by Ashton may have had something to do with it; the basic causes were youth, pride, and incompatibility of interests and temperament. (Walpole after Gray's death stated that the fault was his own, and there is no reason to disbelieve him.) The quarrel, which took place in May, led to an estrangement that lasted until a reconciliation was arranged late in 1745. Thereafter the two were on good terms until Gray's death and corresponded constantly; in fact, now and then Gray did research for some of Walpole's projects. But the two were never quite as intimate as before.

Gray returned alone to England in September, 1741. During the next year he decided to settle in Cambridge—first at Peterhouse, where he had studied, later (1756) at Pembroke College—since living would be inexpensive there and the facilities for study adequate. Save for occasional tours of the countryside, visits to friends and to London, he spent almost all of his remaining life in Cambridge. In 1742 his closest friend, Richard West, died unexpectedly. This tragedy, coupled with the realization that his father's mismanagement of the family finances before his death had left them in a precarious state, contributed to the melancholy which Gray occasionally showed during the succeeding years. In 1742 he greatly increased his writing of English verse. Earlier, almost all his poetry had been in Latin (some of such quality that he is now regarded as one of the best Anglo-Latin poets), but turning to English, he produced with unaccustomed rapidity the *Ode on the Spring,* the *Ode on (Hymn to) Adversity,* and the *Ode on a Distant Prospect of Eton College.* With the exception of the *Elegy* (publ. 1751), most of his English poetry after 1742 fell into two categories. The first was a type which, to some extent, grew out of his interest in medieval history and literature. Examples are the two Pindaric odes (*The Progress of Poesy* and *The Bard*) and several other poems either paraphrased from or inspired by Welsh and Old Norse poetry—*The Triumphs of Owen, Conan, Caradoc, The Descent of Odin, The Fatal Sisters.* The most famous of these, the two Pindarics, were attempts to do something very difficult: to treat literary and political history through an English version of an elaborate classical metric form. They are highly ingenious and show remarkable mastery of metric and onomatopoeic devices, but they do not attain the ease of manner which Gray would have preferred and which one finds in much of the *Elegy.* Samuel Johnson wrote of these works: ". . . in all Gray's odes there is a kind of cumbrous splendour which we wish away"; "His art and his struggle are too visible, and there is too little appearance of ease and nature" (*Life of Gray*). Gray himself sardonically called them "high Pindarick[s] upon stilts" (Letter to Walpole, July, 1752). The second type of poetry—clearly realistic and contemporary in form and mood—was one which seems to have come more easily to him. Two examples are *The Candidate,* a savage personal satire upon that unsavoury peer, Lord Sandwich, and the *Ode on the Death of a Favourite Cat,* one of the most delightful and skillful "mock-odes" of the eighteenth century.

Apart from poetry, Gray devoted most of his life and energy to his studies. Like Milton and Coleridge, he was one of the most learned of the English poets. He had read widely in natural history and his notebooks contain much on insects and meteorology. His knowledge of history, literature, and foreign languages was remarkable. Philosophy, arts, and—not least of all—cooking interested him as well. But though he collected copious notes and was well equipped to write authoritatively in several fields, he never actually settled down to publishing in any of them. He did at one time plan a history of English poetry and wrote a few essays for it, but abandoned the project when he learned that Thomas Warton was working on a similar book. The scattered passages in his letters and the essays in his Commonplace Book[1] show him to have been one of the best English critics of his century, quite capable of producing a history superior to Warton's—but it remained, like so much else in Gray's career, unfinished.

Meantime, Gray unknowingly achieved distinction in another field. He did not write his letters to be published but, like many eighteenth-century correspondents, he knew that his friends might sometimes pass them along to others and he consequently took some pains with them. The scope of Gray's letters is not as broad as that of Walpole, the greatest of all English letter writers, but he is equally amusing and more intellectual. His correspondence is one of the four or five finest in the language.

Gray was reserved in behavior,[2] shy and silent when among people he did not know or like. His restrained and overly fastidious manner sometimes annoyed strangers. Yet there has been too much emphasis upon this side of his character. His friends found him a thoroughly entertaining companion. If he had a melancholy bent and seemed too much concerned with his health, this might have been due to the chronic kidney disease which is thought to have killed him and which may have manifested itself sooner than his biographers realize. It is true that he had a horror of fire which led him to install an improvised "fire-escape" in his rooms at Peterhouse, but this was not necessarily the "morbid fear" of which some scholars have spoken. In 1748, property which Gray owned in London had burned down; his Cambridge rooms were far above ground, in a highly inflammable college

---

[1] Now in Pembroke College Library, Cambridge. Many of the prose sections of the Commonplace Book were edited by C. S. Northup in Gray's *Essays* (Boston: D. C. Heath & Co., 1911). An entirely new edition is now being prepared for the Clarendon Press by A. A. Macdonald. See also Herbert W. Starr, *Gray as a Literary Critic* (Philadelphia, 1941).

[2] Two excellent general accounts of Gray's personality and interests are by W. P. Jones, "Mute Inglorious Gray," *Emory University Quarterly*, XI (1955), 199–207, and by J. W. Krutch in his introduction to Gray's *Selected Letters* (New York: Farrar, Straus and Young, Inc., 1952).

building heated by open fireplaces, illuminated by candles, and inhabited by undergraduates of dubious sobriety. In view of these conditions, anyone who has seen the precipitous drop from Gray's window to the ground will not find his uneasiness surprising. That he did not write and publish more is regrettable, considering his great gifts, but it need not puzzle us. His tastes were not expensive, and his income, if small, was adequate. Though perhaps unduly influenced by the opinions of his friends when they censured his poetry, he felt considerable contempt for the literary taste of the general public, disliked publishing for money and shunned the attendant notoriety. Finally, he was a rather indolent man who needed a definite incentive to embark on any major undertaking.

For all this, it would be wrong to think of Gray as merely a shy recluse of melancholy temperament fitting the popular romantic concept of a poet. His letters show a decided toughness of spirit and a vigorous sense of humor, both bawdy and sardonic.

Literary Background

The *Elegy Written in a Country Churchyard* is best seen in relation to certain poetic types or traditions which were very much alive in the first half of the eighteenth century.[3] One type is "landscape" poetry. Here the poet embodied his philosophic reflections in a scene of nature or the countryside, often described in a generalized way. Both Thomson's *Seasons* and Pope's *Windsor Forest* can be placed in this category. "Graveyard" poetry, a subdivision of this group, differed in being more melancholy and more subjective, as in Edward Young's *Night Thoughts,* which appeared during the period when Gray was probably starting to compose the *Elegy.* Some of this "mortuary" verse gave an almost ludicrous emphasis to death, graveyards, and grotesque "Gothic" gloom. Thus Robert Blair writes, with some zest, in *The Grave* (often published as a companion poem to the *Elegy*):

> The sickly taper
> By glimmering through the low-brow'd misty vaults,
> (Furr'd round with mouldy damps and ropy slime)
> Lets fall a supernumerary horror,
> . . . .
> Midst skulls and coffins, epitaphs and worms:
> . . . .

[3] For more detailed examinations of the literary background, two of the older studies are still useful: Amy Louise Reed, *The Background of Gray's Elegy* . . . (New York: Columbia University Studies in English and Comparative Literature, XXXV, 1924), and Eleanor M. Sickels, *The Gloomy Egotist* . . . (New York: Columbia University Press, 1932).

> In grim array the grisly spectres rise,
> Grin horrible. . . .
> Again the screech-owl shrieks: ungracious sound!
> I'll hear no more; it makes one's blood run chill.

(ll. 16–44)

The *Elegy* belongs to the Graveyard School but is by no means typical of it, for Gray has eliminated—or at least greatly muted—the Gothic touch.

Another traditional literary type, the funeral elegy, had been common in the classical poetry so well known to educated eighteenth-century readers. The elegy usually commemorated a specific death. Elegiac passages appear even in the *Iliad,* and in the later classical period the elegy occasionally merged with both love poetry and pastoral poetry. The pastoral dealt with countryfolk—commonly shepherds and shepherdesses—in a manner customarily idealized but sometimes realistic. When the elegy took on a pastoral framework, it frequently adopted the convention of treating the dead man as a shepherd, mourned by other shepherds, one or more of whom commemorated him in the poem. It normally followed a fairly fixed plan: statement of subject, lamentation, and consolation. The love elegy often departed much further from the original funeral concept by being little more than an ordinary love poem making some use of elegiac trappings to praise a real or imaginary mistress. (The translations of two such elegies by Propertius are among Gray's earliest English poems.) The revival of interest in classical literature during the Renaissance naturally led to a revival of all forms of the elegy. Milton's *Lycidas,* the most famous of the formal pastoral funeral elegies in English, could not help but influence Gray. (See Ellis, pp. 51–62.) Furthermore, just as the landscape poem introduced philosophic musings into a description of scenery, it was not unknown, as we may see in *Lycidas,* for ethical and philosophic problems to be discussed in the elegy.

For his pentameter quatrain, Gray may owe something to James Hammond's *Love Elegies* (published late in 1742 but dated 1743), though by the 1740's this was already a well established verse form. Parallels in phrasing have also been cited between William Shenstone's *Elegies* written (largely in the 1740's) and Gray's poem, but since Shenstone's elegies were not published until long after 1751 and the two men were never acquainted, the resemblances are probably coincidental.[4] Gray, like the bee in Swift, drew his materials everywhere, but the poem he created remains distinctively his own.

[4] See J. Fisher, "James Hammond and the Quatrain of Gray's *Elegy*," *Modern Philology*, XXXII (1935), 301–10, and "Shenstone, Gray and the 'Moral Elegy'," *ibid.*, XXXIV (1937), 273–94.

Composition and Text[5]

It is not known when Gray began the *Elegy*. William Mason (who did not meet Gray until about 1747) was "inclined to believe" that the poem was begun in 1742. Walpole, the more reliable of the two in factual matters, thought 1745 or 1746 more probable. Among modern editors, Toynbee and Whibley,[6] who have carefully reviewed the evidence, favor the later date. In any event, 1746 is the latest probable year, for in a letter of September 11, 1746, Gray mentions "a few autumnal Verses," a description which most scholars believe refers to an early draft of the *Elegy*.

From a knowledge of Gray's habits one may be certain that he polished and revised the poem often and carefully, if at long intervals. The surviving evidence shows that it passed through at least two principal stages. The first is the version entitled "Stanzas wrote in a Country Churchyard," which appears in the Eton MS (sometimes called the Fraser MS, now at Eton College). The second, entitled "Elegy . . ." is found in two later manuscripts (the "Pembroke MS" in Gray's Commonplace Book, now at Pembroke College, Cambridge University, and the Wharton MS, now in the British Museum) and in the final published version in Bentley's *Designs* (1753) and Gray's *Poems* (1768). The variants of the second version preserve many minor revisions that indicate the care Gray gave to both sense and sound effects, but none of these have major importance for questions of interpretation. The case is different with the "Stanzas," [7] where the poem concludes as follows:

[5] A very good discussion of the *Elegy* and its background is George Sherburn's introduction to the Augustan Reprint Society's (No. XXXI) facsimile of the first edition (Los Angeles: William Andrews Clark Memorial Library, University of California, 1951).

[6] Toynbee and Whibley, *Correspondence* (see Bibliography, p. 119), III, Appendix I, 1214–16. The question is of some interest to those who wish to discover what events in Gray's life may be reflected in the *Elegy*. If one wishes to see Richard West consciously or unconsciously portrayed in the "Youth to Fortune and to Fame Unknown" of the "Epitaph," the earlier date is more satisfactory, since West died in 1742. On the other hand, if the trial of the rebel lords is felt to be a crucial element in the poem's genesis (see Newman, pp. 18ff.), the 1745–46 date is preferable —especially since by that time Gray could easily have read Hammond's quatrain elegies.

[7] Minor but interesting variations are to be found in ll. 57, 59, 60, where *Cato, Tully,* and *Caesar* appear instead of the later version's *Hampden, Milton,* and *Cromwell.* It may be added that a student who consults exact reproductions of manuscripts of the *Elegy* should not, unless he makes a most intensive study of Gray manuscripts in general, attach much significance to the peculiarities of Gray's capitalization and punctuation. As may be seen even in the quotations from the

The thoughtless World to Majesty may bow
Exalt the brave, & idolize Success
But more to Innocence their Safety owe   75
Then Power & Genius e'er conspired to bless

And thou, who mindful of the unhonour'd Dead
                        eir
Dost in these Notes thy artless Tale relate
By Night & lonely Contemplation led
To linger in the gloomy Walks of Fate   80

Hark how the sacred Calm, that broods around
Bids ev'ry fierce tumultuous Passion cease
In still small Accents whisp'ring from the Ground
A grateful Earnest of eternal Peace

No more with Reason & thyself at Strife;   85
Give anxious Cares & endless Wishes room
But thro' the cool sequester'd Vale of Life
Pursue the silent Tenour of thy Doom.

Later Gray amended the Eton MS so as to accord more or less
with his final version, except for three alterations. In l. 77 above, "And
thou" was changed to "For thee." After l. 80 the following stanza
was inserted:

If chance that e'er some pensive Spirit more,
By sympathetic Musings here delay'd,
With vain, tho' kind, Enquiry shall explore
Thy once-loved Haunt, this long-deserted Shade.

(This passage ultimately was compressed into the familiar text of
the poem.) After l. 100, a stanza was inserted and then deleted:

Him have we seen the Green-wood Side along,
While o'er the Heath we hied, our Labours done,
Oft as the Woodlark piped her farewell Song
With whistful Eyes pursue the setting Sun.

One other important textual insertion was made. After the publication of the first edition of the *Elegy* Gray added this quatrain (often
referred to as the "Redbreast" stanza) following l. 116 of the standard
version:

Eton MS, Gray's habits in such matters were often inconsistent and careless, and by
no means agreed with the practices of eighteenth-century printers. Indeed he seems
to have taken for granted that the printer would "regularize" his capitalization
and punctuation.

> There scatter'd oft, the earliest of the Year,
> By Hands unseen, are Show'rs of Violets found:
> The Red-breast loves to build, & warble there,
> And little Footsteps lightly print the Ground.

In 1753 he decided to remove these lines, and they do not appear in later texts.

Publication and Reception

It is debatable whether Gray ever intended to publish the *Elegy*, but through Walpole's enthusiasm an imperfect copy found its way into the hands of the editors of the *Magazine of Magazines*. Gray had a very low opinion of this journal, and consequently when he learned that the *Elegy* was to be published in it, he arranged, through Walpole, to have the verses hurriedly printed by Robert Dodsley on February 15, 1751, one day before they came out in the *Magazine of Magazines*.[8]

The reception was enthusiastic by both the critics and the general public. Quite apart from other reprintings, five of Dodsley's editions were required in 1751 alone. The poem became so immensely popular —and retained its popularity with such success for two centuries— that it is still frequently referred to, with some truth, as the best known poem in the English language. By 1946 there had been over 200 English and American imitations and parodies,[9] besides translations into Armenian, Bohemian, Czechoslovakian, Danish, Dutch, French, German, Greek, Hebrew, Hungarian, Icelandic, Italian, Japanese, Latin, Portuguese, Russian, Spanish, and Welsh. In some of these languages (*e.g.*, French, Italian, and Latin) there appear to have been as many as 25 to 40 different renderings. For a poem of only 128 lines, its impact has obviously been enormous.

Many reasons have been advanced for the sudden and sustained popularity of the *Elegy*. The most obvious one is the simple fact that it is an excellent poem. As many critics have said, from the standpoint of sheer poetic technique it is remarkable. The dignified iambic pentameter measure, combined with the skillful use of monosyllabic words

---

[8] When the first edition was published Gray directed that the poem should be printed "without any Interval between the Stanza's [*sic*] because the Sense is in some Places continued beyond them." His instructions were followed (although the first line of each quatrain was indented), but the intervals appear in the editions of 1753 and 1768, in which he had a hand. He either forgot about the matter or decided that it was not important.

[9] See the Northup and Starr bibliographies (p. 119) and W. P. Jones, "Imitations of Gray's Elegy, 1751–1800," *Bulletin of Bibliography*, XXIII (Jan.–Apr., 1963), 230–32.

and long vowels, gives exactly the effect of quiet melancholy for which the poet strives: "And l*e*aves the world to d*a*rkness and to m*e*" (l. 4). Onomatopoeia unobtrusively stresses the background of country sounds: "the beetle wheels his droning flight" and the bells of the sheep are *"drowsy tinklings"* which *"lull* the distant folds" (ll. 7–8). Alliteration is not merely an extraneous ornament; it is used to link words which Gray wishes the reader to associate closely: "The *p*lowman homeward *p*lods his *w*eary *w*ay" (l. 3). Very possibly influenced by Pope's superb use of balanced phrases, Gray often employs parallel structure to heighten his emotional effects. His use of the device varies from the simple balancing of the first half of l. 33 ("The boast of heraldry") against the second half ("the pomp of pow'r") to an elaborate combination of parallels. Stanza V opens with two lines which are parallel statements, follows them with a third line which, deftly avoiding the monotonous sequence of three parallel lines, balances the first half of the line against the second half, and ends with a line which breaks away from the series and grimly summarizes the preceding material:

> The breezy call of incense-breathing Morn,
> The swallow twitt'ring from the straw-built shed,
> The cock's shrill clarion, or the ecchoing horn,
> No more shall rouse them from their lowly bed.

Inverted sentence structure intensifies many of the more important passages—and in the particular instance quoted below causes careless readers to assume that ll. 33–34 are the subject of the singular verb *awaits:*

> The boast of heraldry, the pomp of pow'r,
> And all that beauty, all that wealth e'er gave,
> Awaits alike th' inevitable hour.

From line 28 to line 76 the accomplishments and the graves of the humble villagers are skillfully and elaborately contrasted with the cathedral tombs and the deeds of the worldly great. The contrast is an ironic one, for the poor may have been as talented as the great and might have achieved as much fame if they had been given the opportunity. Yet there is no false sentiment; the poet is quite aware that the circumstances of the poor not only checked "Their growing virtues, but their crimes confin'd" (l. 66). Furthermore, the contrast between the humble and the great is subtly stressed by the use of everyday words to describe the villagers: "For them no more the blazing hearth shall burn,/Or busy housewife ply her evening care" (ll. 21–22); and more formal, almost pretentious, expressions to describe the great: "The boast of heraldry, the pomp of pow'r" (l. 33).

To these and other technical devices, Gray, like Shakespeare and Pope, adds an individual talent which not all good poets possess: the ability to write the striking, highly quotable phrase which expresses so much in so few words. We find it in his other verse: ". . . where ignorance is bliss,/'Tis folly to be wise." (*Eton Ode*, ll. 99–100), but nowhere is it more noticeable than in the *Elegy*. "The short and simple annals of the poor," "Some mute inglorious Milton," and at least a dozen other expressions have become part of our common vocabulary. Probably no other poem of the same length has contributed so many famous phrases to our language.

The importance of this technical mastery must not be underestimated. The bare statement of appealing ideas by themselves has never made a poem great, but when basic emotions and thoughts which we have almost all experienced are expressed with great skill, they move us deeply. For example, the first twelve lines of the poem delicately convey that pleasing sensation of peaceful semi-melancholy so likely to be felt on quiet evenings in the countryside by anyone who does not belong to the rural laboring class. The next stanza smoothly moves to the churchyard where the villagers are buried and provides a link with the description (ll. 17–28) of the simple life of the dead, again a harmonious picture appealing to most sophisticated readers. In the following four stanzas (ll. 29–44) we are more sombrely reminded that the wealthy and the famous have no right to sneer at the humble accomplishments of the countryfolk; fame, wealth, and power also "lead but to the grave." Indeed it may well be that the villagers were as talented as any who were buried with pomp and honor in great cathedrals (ll. 45–75). Here Gray with sound psychological insight skillfully expresses in greater detail our fundamental—if often unjustified—desire to believe that we, too, had we only been granted the opportunity, could have attained far more worldly success. We are convinced that unrecognized talent abounds:

> Full many a gem of purest ray serene,
> The dark unfathom'd caves of ocean bear:
> Full many a flower is born to blush unseen,
> And waste its sweetness on the desert air.

Then, probably to provide a transition (ll. 73–92) to a specific example of unrecognized genius, Gray delicately plays on other fundamental emotions. The fact that this poem really belongs to the elegy tradition is shown by the reference to an individual (the "Youth" of the "Epitaph"). Simple and quiet though the lives of the villagers may be, like everyone else, they wish to leave some memorial behind them, and they quit this world with reluctance:

> For who to dumb Forgetfulness a prey,
> This pleasing anxious being e'er resign'd,
> Left the warm precincts of the chearful day,
> Nor cast one longing ling'ring look behind.

However, sheer literary merit cannot be the only reason for the immediate and continuing popularity of the *Elegy*; other excellent poems are far less well known. Undoubtedly the appeal of the idea content to the era in which the poem was written must be considered. By the middle of the eighteenth century the "Romantic" point of view was beginning to develop, and it remained, in general, the dominant note in poetic style until the 1920's. Thus the *Elegy* with its descriptions of the countryside and its sympathetic, although unsentimental, understanding of rural life at first provided the average reader with something sufficiently new to be stimulating but not so completely unorthodox as to be distressing. For the later reader, who had already accepted the work as a classic, it provided themes, viewpoints, and emotions that were satisfyingly familiar and comprehensible.

Early Criticism of the Elegy

The essays reprinted in this volume have been written in the last twenty-five or thirty years, but they do not exist in a vacuum. They are preceded by nearly two centuries of *Elegy* criticism, and to appreciate fully some of the ideas they express, a reader should have at least a superficial knowledge of the earlier commentary.

In the past, with a few notable exceptions, critics have tended to discuss the poem in such vague and unhelpful terms as "splendid phrasing," "quotability," etc., and to assume that the idea content was almost completely unoriginal and the organization disconnected. However, as Weber (pp. 110ff.) has shown, the fact that the ideas are now familiar to us is by no means an indication that most readers did not find some of them decidedly original in 1751. A characteristic, even more common in Gray's other poetry, which has often been commented on is his use of the "mosaic technique." Like T. S. Eliot, he often echoes phrases that had appeared in earlier poetry. For example, in a footnote to "The Curfew tolls the knell of parting day" Gray himself points out the echo of a passage in Dante, which may be translated thus (The preceding lines in Dante are enclosed in brackets.):

> [It was already the hour which turns back the desire
> Of the sailors, and melts their hearts,
> The day that they have said good-bye to their sweet friends,

> And which pierces the new pilgrim with love,
> If he hears] from afar the bell
> Which seems to mourn the dying day. (*Purgat.* 8. i-vi)

However, these echoes are not invariably conscious in Gray's verse, and, although a knowledge of their sources will probably intensify the reader's pleasure or add a further shade of meaning, recognition of the source and of the original meaning is by no means as essential to an understanding of Gray's poetry as it so often is when studying twentieth-century verse. Occasional objections to the language have been raised. In an article which (although it contains some intelligent criticism) descends to sheer quibbling, an anonymous reviewer in the [London] *Times Literary Supplement*[10] objected to Gray's syntax in the latter part of the poem: "Lines 94–98 do not even make grammar"; " 'Chance' in l. 95 should be understood as meaning 'perchance' "; " 'For thee' and 'thy Fate' [ll. 93, 96] should read 'Of thee' and 'the Fate'. . . . But these 'emendations' would leave the passage in other ways clumsier than ever." The same reviewer expresses the common objection that after l. 76 the poem is loosely organized: "The ideas do not always grow out of each other, or, if they do that, are not always on the right scale." (As the reader will discover, many of the essayists represented in this volume have a very different opinion of the organization.) Yet the dominant attitude toward the *Elegy* from the eighteenth century through the first half of the twentieth century can be seen in two passages which are typical of much *Elegy* criticism in that, although accurate and gracefully expressed, they do not account very searchingly or specifically for the excellence of the poem. The first is from the *Life of Gray* by Samuel Johnson, who strongly disliked Gray and most of Gray's poetry:

> The *Church-yard* abounds with images which find a mirrour in every mind, and with sentiments to which every bosom returns an echo. The four stanzas beginning *Yet even these bones* [ll. 77–92] are to me original: I have never seen the notions in any other place; yet he that reads them here, persuades himself that he has always felt them. Had Gray written often thus, it had been vain to blame, and useless to praise him.

The second passage is by George Sherburn:

> The poem is compact of what Tennyson called "divine truisms" and these are universally, if decorously, affecting. Among poems embodying the noble ideal of "What oft was thought but ne'er so well expressed," [Pope's *Essay on Criticism*, l. 298] this *Elegy* must always rank high. Persons with an aversion to reflective commonplaces in poetry may, as T. S. Eliot has done, question the subtlety of the *Churchyard*; but critics who admit *both*

---

[10] "Gray's Elegy," *TLS*, July 27, 1933, pp. 501–502.

clarity and subtlety as merits will be content with the noble and finished
transparency of this poem. Its achievement is, of its very nature, the opposite of facile: *"divine* truisms" are not so easily come by! [11]

Recently there has been a marked revival of interest in the *Elegy.*
In part this is the reaction to Cleanth Brooks's detailed discussion of
Gray's use of irony not only in the contrast between the villagers and
the famous men who are buried in the cathedral but even in such
paradoxical phrases as "mute inglorious Milton." Whether or not one
always agrees with Mr. Brooks, he is undoubtedly one of the few
critics who have attempted a really intensive analysis of Gray's style
(or at least one aspect thereof) in the *Elegy.* The second cause of the
renewed criticism is the controversy which has developed concerning
the identity of the "Youth" commemorated in the "Epitaph." The
problem is essentially one of pronominal reference. Lines 93–96
read:

> For thee, who mindful of th' unhonour'd Dead
> Dost in these lines their artless tale relate;
> If chance, by lonely contemplation led,
> Some kindred Spirit shall inquire thy fate, . . .

Do the "thee" and the "thy" refer to the author of the *Elegy* (the
Narrator, the "me" of l. 4—*not* the specific individual Thomas Gray
of Cambridge) and the phrase "these lines" to the lines of the *Elegy?*
If so, who relates the Narrator's death in the poem and who writes
the "Epitaph"? Or does the "thee" refer to an imaginary rustic poet
(the "Stonecutter"), an "unletter'd Muse" (l. 81), who wrote epitaphs
("these lines") for dead villagers? If so, is this not a most vague and
strained reference? And, again, who writes the "Epitaph" for him? The
"me" who is the Narrator? And is it not puzzlingly inconsistent to
refer to the Stonecutter-poet in l. 81 as an "unletter'd Muse" and in
l. 119 to write, "Fair Science frown'd not on his humble birth"? In
the first version of the *Elegy* (the "Stanzas") the final reference is clearly
to a Narrator who has written the poem, but this cannot be regarded
as certain proof that Gray did not change his mind in the second
draft. On the whole, a knowledge of Gray's writing habits suggests that
the ambiguity is accidental—and very natural. A man who carefully
revises a poem over several years will devote great thought to such
minute details as substituting "noiseless" for "silent" in "silent tenor"
—doubtless to avoid the clash of two dentals—but will easily overlook
the ambiguity of an important pronominal reference which has always
been clear in his own mind but is not clear to a reader. Undoubtedly

[11] George Sherburn, *The Restoration and Eighteenth Century* . . . [Vol. 3 of
A Literary History of England, ed., A. C. Baugh]. (New York: Appleton-Century-
Crofts, Inc., 1948), p. 1014.

this is a flaw in workmanship, undoubtedly either interpretation is possible, and undoubtedly Gray himself would have been annoyed, amused, and embarrassed by the whole controversy. There is, though, some consolation in the fact that the discussion has at least led to a far greater appreciation of the skillful structure and organization of the *Elegy* than any found in earlier criticism.

Oddly enough, although the poem demonstrates great technical skill, apart from such obvious comments as found in this Introduction (pp. 9–11), the sound effects of the *Elegy* seem to have been the subject of surprisingly little intensive study. There is some excellent discussion in Martin's *Essai* (see Bibliography, p. 120) on pp. 424–36 and in Jack's article in this volume (pp. 88ff.), but more could be done.

In the collection that follows there are necessary and regretted omissions,[12] particularly that of Odell Shepard's "A Youth to Fortune and to Fame Unknown" (*Modern Philology,* XX [May, 1923], 347–73), whose argument that the "Epitaph" was originally a separate poem commemorating Richard West underlies the whole recent "Stonecutter" controversy. A summary, though hostile, of Shepard's article will be found in my own essay. I have sought to present as diverse a group of views as possible, arranged so far as practicable, according to subject matter. Since space is limited, it has been necessary at times to omit or abridge long footnotes. In some of the selections, especially when repetition of material treated elsewhere was involved, passages have been deleted and short summaries substituted. Omissions from the text are indicated by summaries enclosed in brackets or, if no summary is required, by a series of asterisks. The footnotes that accompany the deleted sections have, of course, been omitted as well. When part of a footnote has been deleted the omitted portion has been indicated by marks of ellipsis (thus: . . . .).

---

[12] F[rederick]. W[ilse]. Bateson, *English Poetry: a Critical Introduction* (London: Longmans, Green and Co., 1950), pp. 181–93; Bertrand H. Bronson, "On a Special Decorum in Gray's *Elegy*," in *From Sensibilty to Romanticism* . . ., eds., Frederick W. Hilles and Harold Bloom (New York: Oxford University Press, 1965), pp. 171–76; Frank Brady, "Structure and Meaning in Gray's *Elegy*," *ibid.*, pp. 177–89; Jean H. Hagstrum, *The Sister Arts* . . . Chicago: University of Chicago Press, pp. 292–301; Neil H. Hertz, "Poetry in an Age of Prose: Arnold and Gray," in *In Defense of Reading* . . ., eds., Reuben A. Brower and Richard Poirier (New York: E. P. Dutton & Co., 1962), pp. 65–67; Gilbert Highet, *The Powers of Poetry* (New York: Oxford University Press, 1960), pp. 278–85; I. A. Richards, *Practical Criticism* (London: Kegan Paul, Trench, Trubner & Co. Ltd., 1929), pp. 252–53; Mark Roberts, "A Note on Gray's Elegy," *English Studies*, XXXIX (Dec., 1958), 251–56. (Some of these essays will be reprinted in full or in part in 1968 in a casebook edition of the *Elegy* published by Charles Merrill Books.)

PART ONE

General Criticism

When Curfew Tolled the Knell

by W. M. Newman

When Major-General James Wolfe, moving quietly up the St. Lawrence to his last battle, recited Gray's *Elegy* to his staff, he little thought that it was the Captain-General of the British Army, recently his own chief in the field, who was the true cause of that unique poem.

The story has never before been told, for Gray hushed up the origin of his masterpiece, as he had good reason to do, and but for the work of Professor Tovey it would not have been possible to bring it to light. For Professor Tovey tracked it with great sagacity to August, 1746, but without observing its dependence on the remarkable public events of that month.

Hitherto we have been told that the *Elegy* originated, well, just any how. One version attributed the origin to the death of Gray's aunt. Another, less plausibly, to the death of Uncle Rogers. Another says that he invented the whole thing at Cambridge, that the curfew was St. Mary's, and that the storied urn and animated bust were among the "long-drawn aisles" of King's College Chapel. Presumably the author of that suggestion had never been inside King's. Yet, despite these distractions, Stoke Poges, Bucks., has kept its priority. And no wonder.

What was happening in August, 1746? Well, to begin with, Gray spent the first half of the month in London. There he visited Hampton Court, Richmond, Greenwich, the homes of kings. That he visited Westminster Abbey—where he *would* find storied urns and long-drawn aisles—we do not know, but it is a safe inference, for he is recorded as often visiting Westminster Hall.

Fate at that moment made the deaths of royalties topical, for there died in rapid succession the Kings of Spain and Denmark, and the Dauphiness of France. "We have been a little lucky lately in the deaths of kings," notes Walpole sardonically, and at the end of Gray's

stay the Court went into mourning for two royalties at once, Spain
and the Dauphiness.

All these things, occurring just before a visit to Stoke, might well
seem ample cause for the *Elegy*. But there was more. Gray was of
too cold a temperament to be easily moved to verse. The bell needed
hitting hard before it gave out a musical note, and these were not
hard blows. The crowning cause was an immense national stir, focus-
ing as usual in London, in which the poet was obliged to participate,
firstly by his own nature, secondly by the urgency of his friends, and
thirdly by mere sympathy with the public.

For London was still thrilling with the story of Prince Charlie and
the Forty-five. Only a few months earlier the town had been in fear of
capture, but those fears were dispelled by the artillery of Culloden.
Butcher Cumberland, who left Fort Augustus in mid July, reached
cheering London at the end of the month. Parliament had already
voted him a huge annuity. Handel got busy composing *Judas Macca-
beus* in his honour. It was probably this that started Gray off, for
though no Jacobite, he was no admirer of the German kings; and
Dapper George and the Butcher were far from arousing his enthusiasm
to

> heap the shrine of luxury and pride
> With incense kindled at the Muse's flame.

We read the lines thinking that the muse of poetry is meant, as
Gray knew we should, but there are other muses than she of verse.

During Gray's stay Cumberland was presented with the freedom
of the city in a gold box, while King George himself rode through to
make a speech in the House of Lords, so the poet had ample opportunity to see the objects of his inadequate veneration venerated by others.
He is bound to think, Why don't Authority and Genius praise the
troops also?

> The thoughtless world to Majesty may bow,
> Exalt the brave, and idolise success,
> But more to Innocence their safety owe
> Than Power and Genius e'er conspired to bless.

Had he published his *Elegy* when it was written, had he left that
verse in it, nobody would ever have had any doubt as to what prompted
it. But the *Elegy* was held back for five years, and that verse discreetly
omitted. Had it remained, perhaps George the Third would not have
offered him the Laureateship!

But there was a greater stir in London even than this. It was the
trial in Westminster Hall of the Jacobite peers who had aided Prince
Charlie, a trial which drew most of the *élite*. Gray was there most
days, with his friend Walpole. Here is Walpole's account:

I am at this moment come from the conclusion of the greatest and most melancholy scene I ever yet saw! You will easily guess it was the trials of the rebel Lords. As it was the most interesting sight, it was the most solemn and fine: a coronation is a puppet show, and all the splendour of it idle; but this sight at once feasted one's eyes and engaged all one's passions. It began last Monday; three parts of Westminster Hall were inclosed with galleries, and hung with scarlet; and the whole ceremony was conducted with the most awful solemnity and decency.

Some of these Lords are soon to be beheaded and buried in the Tower. When Gray walks into the Abbey, to mark the fretted vault and hear the pealing anthem he will assuredly glance at the tombs, and make some commonplace reflection that animated busts cannot restore the fleeting breath. Certain lines will now begin to move on his lips. For the wife of the reigning monarch, Queen Caroline, had died a few years earlier, and Gray's dearest friend, Richard West, had written an elegy on her, one of the verses of which is far more applicable to the rebel Lords:

> Ah me! What boots us all our boasted power,
>   Our golden treasure, and our purpled state?
> They cannot ward the inevitable hour,
>   Nor stay the fearful violence of Fate.

Fearful violence does not suit very well for a lady's death bed, but it fits perfectly for the axe and the block. But Gray is bound to see that the first lines are weak, and inveterate critic as he was, begin mending them. Look at this:

> The boast of heraldry, the pomp of Pow'r,
>   And all that beauty, all that wealth e'er gave,
> Awaits alike th' inevitable hour.
> The paths of glory lead but to the grave.

It is doggerel raised to literature. But critic after critic has seen that it was merely West revised.

We have now got our man started. All that is necessary is to carry him to the congenial solitude of the country churchyard and he will finish.

But now came the climax of public tension—the preparations for the execution—the efforts for a reprieve: first this rumour, then that: this Duke interceding—that Countess: this messenger passing—then that. My Lord Cromartie was reprieved. My Lord Kilmarnock was not. My Lord Balmerino harangued the populace from his window: the window was stopped up. And so on till the grim day of the scaffold. Had Gray stayed in town through the climax, he would have been emotionally exhausted by the time he went down to Stoke and would never have written a line more. But—he went down to Stoke while all this was at the height, and there he stayed: his body in the fields, his heart in London: lines of old verse moving in his head, and several candidates for elegics waiting for their doom.

Even that was not all. Fate neglected no means. Gray was a chilly mortal: his circulation was sluggish. Had he sat shivering amid the rigours of an English summer we might have heard no more of it. No sun, no churchyard, no *Elegy*. But the summer was hot. In southern England only half an inch of rain fell in August, and cattle plague broke out. Now, if Gray was sitting in the churchyard when darkness fell, then the weather *must* have been warm. Those of us who live in the country know that it is normally not feasible to sit out of doors after dark in May, or often even in June, while in July and August there is only a moderate chance. And if darkness fell by nine, as Gray implies, then it *was* August. And if the ploughman was coming home, then the crops were in: it had been an early harvest. Which is perhaps also indicated by the sheep bells, possibly folded on the stubble.

Anything else? Yes, the moon. Well, in mid August 1746 the moon was waxing: there she was, silvering the old church tower. It would need a good search through the calendar to match this perfect combination of circumstances. I don't think it can be done.

The rebel Lords were executed at noon on Monday, August 18, on Tower Hill. Gray had been at Stoke about a week. His post town, Slough, is 24 miles from London, so the news will be there during the afternoon, and may well reach Stoke by teatime. August 18 then, equals August 29 modern G.M.T.; sunset is at seven, twilight ends before eight, and night proper begins just before nine. Windsor curfew goes at eight. And the moon is a day from the full.

Everything is as Gray paints it. Presumably he composed a few verses during the failing light. When curfew sounds, he is bound to think that it is doubly a knell, for brave day and braver men. It is a good introduction to his theme, and authors don't often write the first verse first. Here is Gray with a few lines in his notebook, and this is Fate writing the rest: he had only to take them down. He must have been ready to go indoors by 9 P.M.

In view of this abundance of evidence, I doubt whether even the hardiest critic will again seek other sources for the *Elegy*.

A few remaining items may now be cleared up.

> Th' applause of list'ning senates to command,
> The threats of pain and ruin to despise——

Who is this? In his draft Gray blandly elsewhere inserted references to Cæsar and Cicero, and it has been thought that he had some other old Roman in mind here. It is a suggestion worthy of pedantry. That spring the greatest orator of the age, Pitt himself, had been forced into power by public pressure, against the wishes of the Court party, who had tried to ruin him. No need to look through the classics!

> To scatter plenty o'er a smiling land—

Who is this? Presumably that great financier, Sir Robert Walpole, the father of Gray's closest friend. No need to look in Plutarch!

And who is it that wades through slaughter to a throne? Well, Frederick miscalled the Great had just been at it, Bonny Prince Charlie had tried it, and the Bourbons were at that moment doing it. The thing was becoming a habit.

Gray ended up with an apostrophe to himself:

> By night and Lonely Contemplation led
> To linger in the gloomy walks of Fate.

Clever phrase, applicable alike to the Tower and the darkening churchyard.

> Hark how the sacred Calm, that broods around
> Bids every fierce tumultuous Passion cease.

Stoke fierce? Gray tumultuous? No, the rebels and the crowd.

> No more with Reason and thyself at Strife
> Give anxious Cares and endless Wishes room.

So the wishes for a reprieve were against reason? They were.

It is the same formula throughout, Stoke the foreground, London the background.

Had he printed the poem forthwith as it stood, nobody would ever have been in doubt. But he was too astute for that. We can tell what he did, because *we possess his MS.*

He added 16 stanzas, mostly about epitaphs. When? Well, it was several years later, because the first part has considerably faded. Moreover, his handwriting has somewhat changed, he now takes less room for a stanza. Apart from a score of lines which have long provided quotations, their chief interest is in the picture they give of the poet as he lived, out in the early morning, round the high fields, by the greenwood, or recumbent at noon under the beech's old fantastic roots. But it is a full summer picture. As it happens there is no trouble in dating this appendix. The poem was published in the spring of 1751, so it was before that date. In the preceding summer Gray visited Stoke, and his aunt had just died.

I am indebted to the Meteorological Office for the information that the first week of that June was wet, but it turned fine on the 7th, and on Friday the 8th, and Saturday the 9th became blazing hot, thunderstorms following on Sunday.

So we find him on Tuesday, June 12, 1750, writing to Walpole that he has been at Stoke a few days, and has completed a poem begun long before. Almost the next thing we hear is that the *Elegy* is being arranged for the Press. If there *is* anything else that needs explaining, I can't think of it.

Gray's Storied Urn

by Cleanth Brooks

[Brooks explains that the *Elegy* is often regarded as a straightforward piece of writing in which the prose-sense is the main source of the reader's aesthetic response. This is doubtful. The poem, like *The Waste Land,* is "a tissue of allusions and half-allusions." The description of the churchyard and of the dead is not particularly specific. The poem is not a simple mood piece. In fact, much of the effect is gained by the use of ironic contrast.]

Indeed, one can go further. The churchyard is described for the most part, not directly, but by contrast with its opposite: the great abbey church. And there are actually more references to the details of the abbey church as a burial place than to the details of the country churchyard itself.

This becomes plain when we see that the personifications are actually the allegoric figures, beloved by the eighteenth century, which clutter a great abbey church such as that at Bath or at Westminster. It is true that Gray does not restrict himself to the sculptured figures of Memory, Honor, Knowledge; and it is true that he calls some of them by their less flattering names: Ambition, Grandeur, Flattery, Luxury, Pride. But we recognize them clearly enough, even so. They wear the glazed "disdainful smile" of eighteenth-century mortuary sculpture. They take up the conventional attitudes of such sculpture: one leans to soothe the ear—one unrolls the lettered scroll. They are to be met with

> Where thro' the long-drawn isle and fretted vault
> The pealing anthem swells the note of praise.

The marks of their identification seem plain enough. Even so, some readers may hesitate to accept it. Was Gray actually conscious of such a purpose? Is not such a device too witty, too ingenious for a poet of Gray's sensibility? But this is, if not to beg the question, at least to ask

"Gray's Storied Urn." From The Well Wrought Urn, *by Cleanth Brooks (New York: Harcourt, Brace & World, Inc.; London: Dennis Dobson, Ltd., 1947), pp. 96–113. Copyright © 1947 by Cleanth Brooks. Reprinted by permission of the publishers.*

the question badly: for the self-consciousness of the artist is not necessarily involved. The appeal is to be made to the poem itself.

The rural graveyard in its simplicity calls up for the speaker memories of another kind of burial-place, one in which heraldry visibly makes its boast, and one filled with "storied urn" and "animated bust." "Honour," at least, it must be granted, is treated as one of the personifications on an allegorical monument:

> Can storied urn or animated bust
> Back to its mansion call the fleeting breath?
> Can Honour's voice provoke the silent dust . . .

But whether we treat the personifications as sculptures, or as terms used in the grandiloquent epitaphs, or merely as the poet's own projections of the pomp implied by the ornate burial-place—in any case, they are used ironically. That is to say, they are contrasted with the humble graves of the country churchyard, and they are meant, in contrast, to seem empty, flat, and lifeless. For "Honour" to possess more vitality as a metaphor would run counter to the intention of the poem. We can put the matter in this way: the more richly and dramatically realized Honour becomes, the more plausible it would be to feel that "Honour" could "provoke the silent dust." Conversely, the more fully dead, the more flatly abstract Flatt'ry is, the more absurdly ironical becomes its attempt to "sooth the dull cold ear of Death." (There is, of course, here a further level of irony: Flatt'ry attempts what it cannot perform; but further, it is witless in its attempt to do what has already been done: the ear has been fully "soothed" already.)

Once we see that the purpose of the poem demands that the personifications be used ironically, one is allowed to see some of the supporting ironical devices. They are rich, and some of them are intricate. For example, the speaker asks Ambition not to mock the rustics' "homely joys." "Homely" would mean primarily "concerned with the home"— the children running to "lisp their sire's return"—with which the speaker has dealt in an earlier stanza. But "homely" probably still had the meanings (still preserved in America though it has died out in England) of "plain," unadorned. (Milton used it in this sense, and Shakespeare clearly employs it.)

Grandeur is not to smile at the "short and simple annals of the poor." Properly speaking, of course, the poor do not have "annals." Kingdoms have annals, and so do kings, but the peasantry does not. The choice of the term is ironical, and yet the "short and simple" records of the poor are their "annals"—the important records for them.

A more important and brilliant example of such irony occurs in the eleventh stanza. An "animated" bust would presumably be one into which the breath of life had been breathed—a speaking likeness, endowed by the chisel of the sculptor with the soul itself. But the most "animated" bust (*anima* = breath, soul) cannot call the fleeting *anima* of the dead man back to its "mansion." And the mansion receives its qualification in the next line: it is no more than silent dust.

Mr. William Empson has commented on the function of the images in the famous fourteenth stanza: [See Empson selection, p. 109, from "What this means . . ." to ". . . inevitability of death."]

As a counterpoise to the conventional view which sees in the gem-flower comparison only "decoration," this is excellent. But Empson, in his anxiety to establish the "latent political ideas," has extended the implications a little further than the total context of the whole poem warrants. How the implications of the jewel-flower metaphors are qualified by the total context will be discussed a little later.

For the present it will be better to consider the further development which the metaphors receive in the next stanza. The arrangement of the three instances is more subtle than it may at first glance seem. The "prose-sense," of course, is clear enough: a village-Hampden is a Hampden *in petto;* a mute Milton, a man with the potentialities of a Milton without Milton's achievement; and the Cromwell of the case, one who had the potentialities of a Cromwell but who did not realize Cromwell's crimes. But the stanza suggests much more, and qualifies the prose-sense greatly. As we have already remarked, the three names really form a very cunningly contrived scale. We easily accept the "village-Hampden," for his case is proved, and the comparison involved is a rather obvious one. He protests against tyranny, and thus is a petty Hampden, a "village" Hampden. We accept it the more readily because the implication that the village-Hampden might have, had fate placed him on a larger stage, been Hampden himself, is not pressed. But our acceptance of this case carries over to the next where it may help to secure conviction for the claim that the "mute inglorious Milton" might possibly have achieved Milton's glory had "Chill Penury" not "repress'd" his "noble rage"—though here there is no achievement— merely potential achievement, to be accepted on faith. The Cromwell example is, of course, the boldest item and makes most demand upon our acceptance. Here not even potentiality is stressed, but rather the negative virtues, the freedom from the Cromwellian crimes. We are asked to accept the fact that "the guiltless Cromwell" might have realized the virtues *because* the non-realization of the crimes is proved.

The last line goes on to suggest the essentially ironical observation that there can be no *real* Cromwell without blood-guilt. This last point is very pertinent to the argument which the following stanzas make: that the village Hampdens and Cromwells, had not "Their lot forbad," might well have indulged in the worst of "heroic" crimes—waded through slaughter to a throne—or, that the mute inglorious Miltons might have committed the worst of artistic sins—might have heaped

> . . . the shrine of Luxury and Pride
> With incense kindled at the Muse's flame.

It is true, of course, that the speaker does not insist that this would have been the inevitable course that they must have taken had not their "lot forbad." The speaker has admitted that they possessed "growing virtues" to be "circumscrib'd" as well as "crimes" to be "confin'd." Yet the implied judgment is severely realistic: many of the "rude Fore-fathers" would have ended in cruelty and empty vanity had they "learn'd to stray" into the "paths of glory." The paths of glory lead but to the grave, but so does the path along which the "plowman home-ward plods his weary way." The graves are different, as we have seen. But both are graves—the fact of death cannot be glossed over—this is the matter on which Gray's irony exerts its force: not on the senti-mental matter which would try to make of the plowman's "narrow cell" something less than a grave.

One last point before we leave this subject of what the "rude Fore-fathers" might have become. The poet says that "Their sober wishes never *learn'd* to stray." This constitutes a careful inversion of the usual terms. One expects straying to be "natural," not something to be learned. One "learns" to *refrain* from straying. Knowledge has there-fore conferred a favor, whatever her intentions, in refusing to unroll "to their eyes her ample page." For what Knowledge has to give is associated with madness, not sobriety. The rustics' wishes need no sobering discipline—they are already sober; "knowledge" would drive them into ignoble competition with the rest of the "madding crowd." The description of the page of Knowledge as "Rich with the spoils of time" is not literary decoration. It is appropriate and it distinguishes Knowledge as most men know it from the Science which we shall meet with at the close of the poem.

Yet we misread the poem if we conclude that Gray is here merely anxious to insist for the villagers as for the Eton schoolboys, that where "Ignorance is bliss/ 'Tis folly to be wise." He has not overly insisted upon their joys. The portrayal of them has been realistic, not senti-mental. And it has been impossible for them to be wise: it has not been a matter of volition at all: "Their lot forbad. . . ." We shall not come to an instance of choice until we come to the case which concludes the poem.

But if the poem thus far has tended to contrast the country church-yard and the abbey tombs, with the twentieth stanza the two are drawn together once more. The contrast gives perspective to the rustic church-yard, but the comparison is used fairly. The abbey burial ground is, in its turn, humanized by the churchyard. Even the extravagancies on which the poet has looked sardonically are rooted finally in something so deep that it can be found in the country churchyard too: the churchyard has its memorials, though "frail," its rhimes, though "uncouth," and its sculpture, though "shapeless." If the passage carries on the contrast between the sumptuous magnificence of the ornate tombs and those other tombs of "this neglected" spot, and thus adds to the pathos of the rustic graves, it tends to account for the ornate tombs by making them, after all, the expression of a basic human impulse. The "Proud," thus, partake of the pathos in a queer, ironical fashion. For their attempts to hold on to "the warm precincts of the chearful day"— attempts which the speaker has shown to be ineffectual—appear the more desperate in proportion as their luxury exceeds the simple tomb.

The Miltonic inversion of the twenty-second stanza supports the effect very nicely. "For who, to dumb Forgetfulness a prey," etc., can mean: for what man, having forgotten himself completely, ever left the cheerful day without casting back a look of regret. Actually most of us will read it as meaning: for what man ever resigned this being as a prey to oblivion without casting back one look of regret. But, on reflection, the two meanings tend to coalesce. To forget one's human nature sufficiently to be able cheerfully to leave the "warm precincts of the chearful day" makes a demand as heroic as that of cheerfully resigning oneself to being forgotten by other men. In either case, one becomes the prey to "dumb Forgetfulness." The general commentary on death (which ends with line ninety-two) has thus brought the proud and the humble together in a common humanity. The impulse to hold on to life—to strive against the encompassing oblivion—is to be found under the "yew-tree's shade" as well as beneath the "fretted vault." If the one has been treated with more pathos, the other with more irony, still neither can be effectual, and both in their anguish of attempt are finally deeply human.

The poet, it seems to me, carries very fairly here between both groups. To press, with Empson, the poet's complacency in seeming to accept the fate of the humble is to ignore these elements in the poem. (Thomas Gray, as a man, may or may not have been guilty of such complacency. But we are not dealing with Gray's political ideas. We are dealing with what the "Elegy" "says"—something that is not quite the same thing.)

Any doubt as to this last point should be dissipated by a consideration of the resolution of the poem. For what is the *speaker's* choice? After all, if the rude Forefathers of the village could not choose, since Knowledge did not unroll her ample page to them, *he* at least can choose. "Fair Science frown'd not on his humble birth." He *need* not be buried in the churchyard in which he actually wishes to be buried.

But before one goes on to examine the significance of his choice, it is well to begin with the first lines of the "resolution." With line ninety-three the speaker comes to apply the situation to himself. He should, therefore, be saying

> For *me*, who, mindful of th' unhonour'd Dead
> *Do* in these lines their artless tale relate;
> If chance, by lonely contemplation led,
> Some kindred Spirit shall inquire *my* fate, etc.

(In the first stanza the speaker was willing to say *me:* "And leaves the world to darkness and to me.") Dramatically, what has happened is that the meditation has gone on so fervently that in talking to himself, the speaker has lost his identity as an ego. The commentary which has been going on, though it has begun as that of the solitary observer, has become more general, more external. It would be a nice point to determine precisely *who* does speak this twenty-fourth stanza: the spirit of the place, the Muse, Melancholy, one side of the speaker's own nature? Presumably, the speaker is a part of the observer's own nature; but in any case, the observer is willing to be addressed in the second person: he is willing to see himself as he shall be, merely one with the others in the country churchyard.

We have said that this last section of the poem is to be considered the resolution of the poem: first, we have had the case of those who could not choose, the "rude Forefathers of the hamlet"; next, the Proud, who chose, but chose in vanity; lastly, there is the present case, the man who is able to choose, and chooses the "neglected spot" after all. But though his choice is a kind of vindication of the lot forced upon the rustics—a point which Empson's discussion of the poet's attitude fails to take into account—still, it will not do to insist upon the speaker's conscious choice lest it seem too smugly heroic; or to make his identification with the rustics too easy, lest it seem unrealistic. It is better that the "I" to be buried should treat that self as passive, as he does. Moreover, stanza twenty-four grows out of the preceding stanza: it is human for the parting soul to wish for an understanding friend:

> E'en from the tomb the voice of Nature cries,
> E'en in our Ashes live their wonted Fires.

The speaker does not attempt to sustain an inhumanly heroic role. He too yearns for "Some kindred Spirit" who shall inquire his fate; and he provides an epitaph to be read by that unknown friend.

Furthermore, he sees clearly that his motives in keeping himself in obscurity—in confining himself to "the cool sequester'd vale of life"—will hardly be understood by the unlettered companions who accompany him through the vale. Their "sober wishes [have] never learn'd" the vanity of straying from it; his, sobered by wisdom, have learned the folly of straying from it. They, saved by ignorance, cannot comprehend his saving knowledge. It is a nice touch, therefore, which has the observer envisage with complete realism the account of him which the "hoary-headed Swain" would necessarily give to the inquirer. To the Swain, he will be a creature pathetically inexplicable, and perhaps crazy:

> 'Now drooping, woeful wan, like one forlorn,
> 'Or crazed with care, or crossed in hopeless love.

It is significant that the hoary-headed Swain cannot read the epitaph which might explain the observer's conduct and his choice. But even if he could read the epitaph, it is evident that he still could not understand it, for the implication is that only a "kindred Spirit" could understand. In its way, then, his own epitaph will be more lonely than the other epitaphs about it—those on which the name and years "spelt by th' unletter'd muse,/ The place of fame and elegy supply."

And what of the epitaph itself? Does it furnish a proper climax for the poem? Or is it, after all, trite, flat, with an eighteenth-century tameness? Landor regarded it as a tin-kettle tied to the tail of an otherwise noble poem; and certainly the epitaph has come in for very little praise ever since the poem was published. But before one undertakes to defend the epitaph as poetry, it is better to make sure first that we understand it—in itself, and in its relation to the rest of the poem.

To take up the first question (for the silence of the commentators here warns us that the explication had better not be taken for granted): what does the epitaph say in itself? In the first place, it implies the choice of which we have spoken in its very first line. His head will be laid upon the "lap of Earth"—the grave will be in the churchyard, not within the church. And the lines that follow have to do with the choice further: he will be unknown, but not because his "lot forbad." Fair Science did *not* frown upon his humble birth, as she has upon the humble birth of his companions in the churchyard. Why does the poet not go on to write: "But Melancholy . . ."? This would be an easier reading: that is, he had the knowledge requisite for entering into the competition for fame, but he was incapacitated by Melancholy. But the poet's choice of the conjunction "and" compels the richer reading: Melancholy is something more than a disease which rendered him unfit for the "madding crowd's ignoble strife." It is associated with "Fair Science," which in turn is differentiated by the association from the earlier "Knowledge" with which we might have been tempted to identify it. Melancholy becomes thus, in association with Science, a kind of wisdom which allows him to see through the vanities which delude the Proud.

"Large was his bounty. . . ." How? Because, like the widow's mite, what he gave to Misery represented his all. How did Heaven render him as largely prosperous? Because Heaven gave him everything that he could possibly wish. Are the oppositions here merely pertly ironical? If we take the epitaph in isolation, perhaps they are. But the ironies of this stanza have the whole of the poem behind them. This epitaph, which the speaker contemplates as one to which the kindred Spirit may be directed by the hoary-headed swain, is to be read in the light of the commentary already made upon those which recite the short and simple annals of the poor, and those others which are dictated by "the pomp of pow'r." This epitaph commemorates one of the literally poor ("all he had, a tear") but it claims to be the epitaph of a man who was rich—in his bounty to the miserable, and in the possessions which Heaven has showered upon him. (If, again, the paradox seem too easy, too brittle, we must in fairness take the stanza in terms of the context already established: there, it has certainly been implied that a true friend is the rarest of things. The trophies which Memory raises over the tombs of the proud admit Flattery to their company.)

And now for the last stanza: is it modesty which requests the reader to seek no farther "his merits to disclose." Two of the "merits" have already been disclosed. Have these two been chosen because they are modest and ordinary, or because they are in reality superlatively rare? If we are alive to the context, we can use both these answers: generosity to the poor and the proofs of Heaven's favor (in accomplishment, in achievement) are the common matter of epitaphs. In this sense, the speaker's imagined epitaph is thus typical and conventional. Yet these "merits" are more often boasted of rather than exemplified.

But there is a better reason still for the choice: the merits disclosed are those which have special reference to the opinion of the world: what Heaven bestowed, and what the recipient himself bestowed to the needy. Thus far the imagined epitaph complies with the demands of the world; for the rest, "his other merits" and his frailties—these have another reference. Knowledge of them is already possessed by the only Being who can judge them and thus the only Being to whom they are pertinent.

Even so, the reader may not be altogether convinced, as I am not altogether convinced, that the epitaph with which the poem closes is adequate. But surely its intended function is clear, and it is a necessary function if the poem is to have a structure and is not to be considered merely a loose collection of poetic passages.

Moreover, it ought to be equally clear that the epitaph is not to be judged in isolation. It is part of a context, and a very rich context. We have to read it in terms of the conditions for a certain dramatic propriety which the context sets up. Among those conditions are these: it must be a recognizable epitaph, even a humble epitaph, modest in what it says, and modest, perhaps, even as an example of art. For it is the epitaph, after all, of a "Youth to Fortune and to Fame unknown." It must be closely related to the evening meditation in the churchyard, for it is an outgrowth of that meditation.

But what, then, of the "kindred Spirit" who may some day read it? How is he, coming upon the epitaph, and reading it, naked of the context of the whole meditation—what is he to be expected to make of it? It is all very well to treat the poem as a dramatic structure, but if we do, then will the epitaph for the "kindred Spirit" incorporate within itself enough of a qualifying context? Or will it not seem to him rather flat and bare? But the poet has evidently taken this question into account. The "kindred Spirit" must presumably know something of the youth, though "to Fortune and to Fame unknown," if he is to be able to inquire about his fate at all. He will come to the epitaph possessed by a proper mood, led to this spot by "lonely contemplation." And the fact that he is a "kindred Spirit" will supply for him much of the context which the poet has elaborately built up for us in the poem itself. Indeed, the poet has prepared us, the readers, to be the "kindred Spirit" if we wish. The poet has been too good a poet, in his practice at least, for him to rely here upon the "prose-sense" of the epitaph as such. Whatever its merit (or lack of merit) as a poem in its own right, it is not the "Elegy written in a Country Churchyard," nor is the reader brought to it in isolation as the "kindred Spirit" may be, nor is Gray merely identical with the youth in the poem who is "to Fortune and to Fame unknown."

In the poem, as we have seen, the epitaph is set over against the "shapeless sculpture" of the churchyard and also over against the "storied urn" of the abbey church. We have tried to see what its relation to each is. But when we come to Gray himself, it is the whole "Elegy" that is *his* storied urn—it is the poem itself, the "lines" in which he relates the "artless tale" of the villagers—all the lines of the poem, the whole poem, taken as a poetic structure. As for the urn which stands beside the "animated bust," its "stories" are supposed to be the material proper to art, and surely, as the speaker of the poem envisages the storied urn, they have been treated artfully—in all the senses of that ambiguous word. By contrast, the "tale" which the speaker of the poem undertakes to relate is, on the other hand, admittedly "artless." It is conventionally regarded as matter which cannot be turned into art. It is artless in this sense because the men whose tale it is were themselves *artless*—too innocent, too simple to have a significant story. Their story is merely a tale; it is no more properly a set of "annals" than the tale of Donne's lovers is properly a "chronicle."

But is Gray's telling of the "artless tale" really artless? The tale is simple enough, to be sure; but is the telling simple: is the structure of the poem simple? Not, most of us will agree, in the sense that it lacks art—not in the sense that it is either a casual collection of poetic "materials" or in the sense that it is the "artless" rendition of a set of poetic truths. The "Elegy" has a structure which we neglect at our peril if we mean to pass judgment on it as a poem, or, even if we are merely to point to it as a poem. It is a "storied urn," after all, and, many of us will conclude that, like Donne's, it is a "well wrought urne," superior to the half-acre tombs of the Proud.

Gray's *Elegy*: "The Skull Beneath the Skin"

by Lyle Glazier

Gray's *Elegy* is sometimes discussed as if its chief aim were to persuade the poor and obscure that their barren lives are meaningful, or, even more unflattering to Gray, as if aimed to persuade the privileged classes (in whose ranks Gray was proud to consider himself) that they need not trouble their consciences over the poor, who have already all essential riches. Actually, equating the lives of rich and poor, famous and obscure, is a large and important part of the poem, but it is part of a still larger statement—that mortality is the essential element of all men, the lowly *and* the great. In this respect, and Gray claims that it is the only respect which finally matters, all men are equal.

In a sense, the interpretation of the poem revolves around placing the emphasis in a single line. It lies in the difference between saying, "The paths of *glory* lead but to the grave," and saying, "The paths of glory lead but to the *grave*." The first is like saying, "Although the paths of glory lead to the grave, the paths of virtue lead elsewhere." The second is like saying, "The paths of glory, and all other paths, lead but to the grave." The first is either a consolation prize held out to the cheated underprivileged, or it is a sop to the chafed consciences of the "enlightened" rich. The second is a reminder to all men that, whatever their achievements, they face a common doom. The first makes Gray out to be a double-talking hypocrite, for who would claim that the man who took such pride in being a gentleman and such pains in being a poet had no consideration for differences in rank and ability? The second makes him out to be an honest man, who recognized the essential paradox of human life—that its deepest core is death, "the skull beneath the skin."

The chief difficulty in interpreting the *Elegy* lies in the fact that the two subjects (1. the poor and obscure are essentially as favored as the wealthy and famous, and 2. death is the common destiny of all men) are overlapping, so that it is easy to make the mistake of thinking

"*Gray's* Elegy: '*The Skull Beneath the Skin*,'" by Lyle Glazier. *From the* University of Kansas City Review, *XIX* (*Spring, 1953*), *174–80. Copyright* © *1953 by* University of Kansas City Review. *Reprinted by permission of publisher.*

that they are synonymous. The difference between them is in fact considerable. The first is chiefly political and social in its implication, the second chiefly religious and philosophical. The first is being dinned into the ears of twentieth-century Americans by many pseudo-patriotic propaganda machines, the second is frequently discussed by our poets. Intelligent readers would prefer to classify Gray with the poets. We have not always done so. Frequently a memorable line or group of lines from the *Elegy* has come to stand for the whole poem.

> Full many a gem of purest ray serene,
> The dark unfathom'd caves of ocean bear:
> Full many a flower is born to blush unseen,
> And waste its sweetness on the desert air.

That stanza has doubtless offered consolation to unnumbered thousands, who have felt the anguish of knowing that their diamond-edged brilliance was undiscovered, or that their flower-like innocence was never smelled out. Gray suffers, like Pope, from having written verbal gems so scintillating that they all but destroy their contexts. From time to time it becomes the critic's function to shift the attention back to the unquoted parts of the poem, even to overemphasize them; otherwise readers, even when they think they are reading the whole poem, will not truly read it, but merely skim the lines in anticipation of the gems.

However much we cling to the concept of Gray as a harbinger of Romanticism (and certainly *The Bard* is a remarkable blend of romantic spirit and classical form), the *Elegy* provides no evidence that Gray's social views were those of a romantic rebel. Neither does it, as Cleanth Brooks believed, show that Gray was a hypocritical social snob. An examination of the *Elegy* as a whole reveals that he considered his generalization about death to be the subject of his poem, while his balancing of privileged and underprivileged is only by way of illustration—carrying his generalization out to its social limits of rich and poor.

A brief outline of the *Elegy*'s main argument reveals the single theme enunciated by every element of imagery in this highly sensuous poem. The poem's first statement, contained in the first four stanzas, is imagistic, developing a picture of night settling down over a solitary watcher in the close, small world of a country churchyard. The essential note is struck in the first line, where day's knell is tolled; *tolls, knell,* and *parting*—in a short line three words convey death's mastery over the atmosphere of the poem. In these first stanzas there is no dramatic balancing of poor and rich, of obscure and famous, as there might have been if Gray had intended to make social criticism his main theme. In stanza four, the last lines conclude the opening picture with a statement which intensifies the concept of death's sovereignty, by reminding the living poet of his proximity to the graveyard, where,

> The rude Forefathers of the hamlet sleep.

The three following stanzas continue to assert the sovereignty of death by telling us that even when alive, the most meaningful fact about the rude forefathers was that they were on the path leading to the grave. Their former activities are described, but from a novel and ironic perspective; like the audience watching the graveyard scene in Thornton Wilder's *Our Town,* we are not permitted to forget that now these actors are dead. "No more"—"For them no more": their knells are tolled throughout the stanzas. Their jocund and sturdy activities are all in the past.

It is only after this full and careful statement of his theme that Gray introduces the balancing of the poor and the rich. He introduces it not as a point of consolation; the crumb of comfort offered the poor is small indeed. Rather, Gray admonishes the rich not to scorn the poor, for all share a common doom. It is not in felicity that the poor are equated with the rich. They are equal in death, the universal "proud brother." Nor does the final section of the poem proper (before the epitaph) emphasize the balancing of social classes. The emphasis is on the pathetic, because futile, ambition of all men to achieve immortality—futile because in the end "Forgetfulness" will claim them.

Finally, the chief significance of the epitaph is that it is a statement about a man who is dead. It illustrates Man's last, and again, futile attempt to avoid oblivion. The fact that the young man for whom the epitaph was written had chosen the obscure life indicates only that he had embraced fully the pessimistic philosophy stated in the poem: death is the common end of all. Why then labor to achieve greatness? It is not particularly significant that Gray, the self-conscious gentleman, renounces aristocracy in writing his own epitaph. The masquerade of aristocrat as proletarian is an easy intellectual feat for a poet familiar with the long classical pastoral tradition: the chief reason why Gray's shepherds are realistic and not idealized is that he wishes to exploit them for self-commiseration, not for escape. The net effect of the whole poem is negative and fatalistic, this in spite of the fact that in the epitaph Gray surprises the twentieth-century reader (anything else would have surprised his contemporaries) by introducing into his bleak universe the Heaven of orthodox Christian faith. This promise of spiritual immortality turns the poem into a medieval rather than a modern statement. It is as if Gray, frightened at his own pessimism, retreated suddenly into the safe haven of medieval theology (the world is vanity, Heaven is all), and shut the door. The spontaneous Gray spoke first; the conventional Gray spoke last. Both speeches are honest, and it is fruitless to argue which came from a greater depth of spirit. It is not fruitless, however, to point out that the promise of Heaven is added to a poem which offers almost nothing in the way of compensation, and that by adding this promise, Gray compromises the integrity of his vision.

A fuller analysis of the poem can merely fill in the outline already given. A stanza by stanza analysis will not shock the modern reader as much as it would have shocked Gray, who preferred to think of his poem as a continuous unit, with no stanzaic divisions. If the poem had always, or ever, been printed as he desired, possibly the integrity of the whole would not have been so easily destroyed, but even the first quarto indicated stanzas by indenting every fourth line.

Part of the business of stanza one is to establish the tone or mood of the poem. Some rather irreverent tampering with the lines will serve to emphasize the mood Gray wished to create. It is possible by three deletions and one unforgivable emendation to illustrate both the redundancy of Gray's language and the perfection of his eye and ear. The stanza can be turned into tetrameters as follows:

> The curfew tolls the knell of day,
> The lowing herd winds o'er the lea,
> The ploughman homeward plods his way,
> And leaves the darkened world to me.

That pat—and flat—stanza shows the folly of arguing that *parting* is a useless epithet for a day whose knell has already been tolled, that no herd could wind homeward any other way than *slowly,* that *weary* is implicit in *plods.* The revised stanza may have a higher specific gravity, since the verbal redundancies have been cleaned out, but the sonority and dignity and the true gravity of idea have suffered. Possibly, octosyllabics could have served Gray as well as pentameters, but it would have had to be a new poem, octosyllabic from the start; cutting this one down destroys the main, atmospheric idea.

Besides establishing atmosphere, the first stanza builds a sensation of a world closing in. There is an imagistic contraction of the landscape in from the horizon. The world is narrowing down toward the final narrow box, though as yet we do not know toward *what.* The last line of the stanza, so insipid in the tetrameters, is in the original a dramatic description of a world gone blank: "And leaves the world to darkness. . . ." Just as the first three lines shrink down a specific landscape, the last line transforms that landscape into an emblem for the world, which is shrunk down too. The last phrase, ". . . and to me," identifies outer and inner darkness; macrocosm is concentrated in microcosm, the universe in Man. Here again, we do not at once know the full meaning of the statement, but it echoes in the mind, and takes on a broader meaning as the poem develops.

The shift from outer darkness to inner darkness involves a shift in dramatic point of view, artfully contrived (at least the result is artful, however spontaneous the contriving may have been) to create in the reader an acceptance of the poem-world as indisputably real. The poem begins omnisciently and objectively with statements of fact: these things happen; they are not *seen,* they *are.* The landscape closes in, the world grows dark and void; it is not until the end of the last line that it closes in on someone. By then it has closed in on the reader also, and the poet observer has completed his identification with the reader. It is every reader, every man, who is shut inside this narrowing universe. What happens in the imagination of this man will be symptomatic of mankind. In his opening stanza Gray has achieved the note of universality so dear to the hearts of his neo-classical contemporaries.

Now, the dramatic point of view has been established: we are viewing the world from the eyes and mind of one man, who is Mankind. His place in the universe is Man's place in the universe. The next three stanzas (2–4) continue to unfold that universe. The Everyman poet-observer has selected a melancholy world to inhabit. It is a solemn, fading world, where faint and transitory sounds serve to intensify the general stillness. It is a world brooded over by the church tower, and inhabited by the grieving owl. Finally we reach the destination toward which we have been moving—the gravcyard "Where heaves the turf in many a mould'ring heap." Our destination is not the collective burial plot but the individual grave: "Each in his narrow cell for ever laid." Gray has now accomplished his first objectives: melancholy has become the atmosphere, and the "narrow cell" the sphere, of Man. Each rude forefather of the hamlet has become a type for mankind. There is thus a double Everyman in the poem—the poet-observer, who is Everyman still alive and reflecting about death, and each rude forefather, who is Everyman already dead and under ground. They merge together later in the poem, when the poet suddenly projects himself into his own grave, and from there reflects about his own hopeless desire for immortality.

The next three stanzas (5–7) recount the imagined activities of each dead man, when he was man alive. Because these activities are engaged in only in the poet's retrospect, because they are recited about men who are already dead, the shadow of inevitable death is carried back into the world of the once living. The chief statement of these stanzas, implicit in the phrases "No more" and "For them no more," is that life is a mere shadow-acting before the coming of death. Death is already in the marrow. Life is not so much a developing, as a peeling off of outer, extraneous tegument until the essential skeleton is exposed.

In stanzas 8–11, Gray brings in for the first time the contrast between the rude forefathers and the ambitious and proud of the world. He does this not to rationalize away the futility of the lives of the poor who have been gathered here into their graves. He is merely extending the domain which he has given to Death. The ambitious and proud need not mock the useful though unheralded toils and joys of these poor dead; the inevitable hour waits for the great man also. Nor can he ward off death by having his story painted on an urn or by paying someone to carve his image in a life-like bust. Just as the preceding stanzas presented the paradox of death in life for the obscure countryman, so these four stanzas present the same paradox for the honored and flattered great. Life is for all an ironic paragraph ending in death.

The next eight stanzas (12–19) merely intensify the poem's fundamental point about death's mastery over life, though we must be careful or our instinctive regret for wasted lives will make us read the stanzas incorrectly. Out of context they seem to say: don't cry over the "village-Hampdens," the "mute, inglorious Miltons," the "guiltless Cromwells" buried here; if they lacked the glories of life, they lacked also its excesses. Actually what is said is: don't cry over the Hampdens, Miltons, Cromwells buried here; if they had been vocal and active, the net result would be the same: death would have them now. Stanzas 17–19, the only truly consolatory stanzas except for the epitaph, come in by way of a natural desire on Gray's part to give both sides of his equation between poor and rich. The consolatory note, though present, is hardly strong enough to upset the whole discourse of the poem. And the consolation is slight. The poor are not congratulated on having equal felicity with the rich; they are congratulated on having avoided some of their excesses. Chiefly, they are informed, as the following stanzas (20–29) show, and as the preceding stanzas (1–11) should have kept us mindful, that they share with the rich, the powerful, and the famous the essential destiny of mankind—the grave—and the essential and tragic ambition of mankind—the desire for self-perpetuation beyond the grave. You need not go outside any social class to find Everyman. Wherever a man lies buried, Everyman lies there.

The desire for self-perpetuation is discussed in general terms, in stanzas 20–23. Just as the shadow of death inhabits life, so the fierce urge to perpetuate life is projected into death. The double irony of Man's existence is exposed in an antithesis which divides the poem into nearly-equal parts—the first part (1–22) governed by the concept of the skeleton beneath the skin, and the second (23–32) governed by the voice of life crying out of the ashes of the dead. The pathetic vanity of Man is now revealed: his heart is set on immortality, but he is "to dumb Forgetfulness a prey." From here on, the poem reiterates the futility of this blind, instinctive urge of man to perpetuate the life that is in him, when what is essentially in him is death; the end of life is death, yet

> Ev'n from the tomb the voice of Nature cries,
> Ev'n in our Ashes live their wonted fires.

And (stanza 24) suddenly, dramatically, in spite of all his rationalizing about vanity, it happens for the poet—or for the poetic mouthpiece, the exemplar of Man, the Everyman of the poem. The voice from the ashes strikes his imagination so keenly that his own human desire for immortality conquers his reason, and in his imagination he is dead and underground, and the voice of Nature is addressing him— "thee" (the poet, still alive, who relates these "artless tales")—and forcing him to express his pathetic urge for self-perpetuation. Just as for the living the most eloquent voice is that of the skeleton within, so for the dead the most eloquent(though doomed) voice is that of life in the marrow of the decomposing bones.

Stanzas 25–29 present a brief parable of the triumph of vanity over even the controlled imagination of the poet. He tries to comfort himself with thoughts of a brief immortality in the memories of those who will outlive him. This is completely pathetic when read in the light of the earlier stanzas with their repeated message: ". . . to dumb Forgetfulness a prey." The poet knows this, knows the futility of trying to extend life; yet his common human vanity is stronger than his intellectual awareness of inevitable oblivion. And when his death is dramatized in his imagination, it is with all the accompaniments of frail humanity; though he has been objective about others, he cannot imagine himself dead without instinctively crying out for self-perpetuation, making the gesture which his intellect has repeatedly told him is futile.

There is, unfortunately, in this last section before the epitaph, a note of mawkish self-pity, which lends weight to the belief that Gray wrote his poem in a fit of self-commiseration to find consolation for the world's neglect. That he consciously avoided notoriety in the publication of his poem does not entirely prove that he did not have moments when he would have enjoyed the world's praise. There is no denying that the self-pity is there. A sheaf of emotional cliches are paraded to wring out sympathy for the youth: he is "drooping," "wan," "forlorn," "craz'd with care," and "cross'd in hopeless love." That the youth is Gray cannot be doubted: who else related the "artless tales" "in these lines"? The line in the epitaph, "He gain'd from Heav'n ('twas all he wish'd) a friend," supports the interpretation that at the end of his poem, Gray used the earlier stanzas to comfort himself with the thought that earthly neglect is inconsequential, considering the common doom of mankind; " 'twas all he wish'd" has the sweet sour note of a miserable Pollyanna. However, the *Elegy* is large enough to endure this sentimental flaw: the reader squirms uncomfortably in his chair and wishes that Gray had been more reticent, but the total effect of the poem, though dimmed, is not obliterated.

The most important thing about the epitaph, as I have already said, is that it is a statement about a man who is already dead. Upon this dead man accumulate all the conditions stated earlier in the poem. These three stanzas are his final bid for immortality. But (discounting Heaven) the bid is doomed, like those of all men buried in country churchyards or storied urns. The paths of glory, and the paths of obscurity, lead but to the grave.

F. G. Stokes, in his study of the first quarto and the manuscripts, notes the emblems, or drawings, which accompanied the first twelve editions of the *Elegy*:

> Two rough wood-blocks, depicting funereal emblems in white on a black ground, are placed the one at the head of the title page, and the other above the imprint. The wood-blocks are in the form of bands about 5 inches long and ½ inch wide, bevelled at the ends like the upper and lower portions of a picture-frame. The emblems are: (upper) *skull, bones, crown, bones, hour-glass, bones, spade, skull,* and (lower) *skull, mattock, bones, hour-glass, bones, crown, bones, skull.*

If these emblems signify anything, they signify that the *Elegy* is not sugar on a rag held out to keep the lower classes contented. Nor is it an *In Memoriam* for Richard West, for Gray's aunt, or for any other person. The *Elegy Written in a Country Church-Yard* is a *memento mori* for the race of Man.

PART TWO

The "Stonecutter" Controversy

"A Youth to Fortune and to Fame Unknown": A Re-estimation

by Herbert W. Starr

In an article entitled "A Youth to Fortune and to Fame Unknown" [1] Professor Odell Shepard advanced the theory that the "Epitaph" appearing at the end of Gray's *Elegy* had originally been written to commemorate Gray's dead friend Richard West and later joined to the *Elegy* by the insertion of several transitional stanzas.

This possibility seems to have aroused little comment until recently. To the best of my knowledge Roger Martin makes no reference to it in his *Essai sur Thomas Gray* and William Powell Jones refers to it only briefly and cautiously in *Thomas Gray, Scholar*: "Characteristically Gray wrote in English a stilted sonnet on West's death and put his genuine feelings into the Latin verses that he appended to his philosophical fragment, *De principiis cogitandi*. Not enough of a romantic to wear his heart on his sleeve, he concealed his emotions in classical Latin until they came out years later, thoroughly fused with the common sorrow of the world, in the *Elegy Written in a Country Churchyard*." [2] Yet despite the rather ambiguous nature of this acceptance we find the following statements appearing in a recent anthology in the section under the editorship of Professor Shepard: In reference to the "him" of l. 98 in the *Elegy*: ". . . usually taken to refer to Gray. More probably the person described in the following lines and in the Epitaph is Richard West." [3] "The fact is

---

"'A Youth to Fortune and to Fame Unknown': A Re-estimation," by Herbert W. Starr. From Journal of English and German Philology, *XLVIII, no. 1 (January, 1949)*, 97–107. *Copyright © 1949 by* Journal of English and German Philology. *Reprinted by permission of the editor.*

[1] *MP*, XX (May, 1923), 347–73.
[2] W. P. Jones, *Thomas Gray, Scholar* . . . (Cambridge, Mass., 1937), p. 8. There follows a footnote referring to Shepard's article.
[3] *The College Survey of English Literature*. B. J. Whiting, F. B. Millett, A. M. Witherspoon, Odell Shepard, A. P. Hudson, E. Wagenknecht, L. Untermeyer, eds.

demonstrable, however, that the last nine stanzas of the poem were written with Richard West in mind. We should not, therefore, read the 'Epitaph' at the end with the awkward, and indeed the rather absurd, supposition that Gray is there referring to himself." [4]

Since this identification appears as a fact in a textbook widely used in sophomore classes throughout the country, it is perhaps time for us to examine somewhat more carefully the evidence upon which it rests. Let us recapitulate Professor Shepard's argument, pausing to note certain objections.

The crux of the entire matter rests upon the questions raised by ll. 93–94 of the *Elegy*: "For *thee* [my italics] who, mindful of the unhonoured Dead,/Dost in *these lines* [my italics] their artless tale relate." Who is the "thee" referred to? Is it the author of the *Elegy* himself or the Youth whose story is told in the following stanzas? Are "these lines" the lines of the *Elegy* or the "uncouth rhimes" which appear on the "frail memorials" and are provided by "the unlettered Muse" (ll. 77–84)? Professor Shepard approaches the problem by stating that there are three possible interpretations of the Youth: (a) "a purely imaginary personification of the type *poeta*"; (b) "an actual poet entirely unknown to fame, an *Ignotus,* whom Gray, however, had known at Stoke Poges or elsewhere"; (c) "Thomas Gray himself." [5] Now it is vital to his argument that these three possibilities be accurately defined and completely eliminated, for only by doing so can he prove that a fourth interpretation—West—is the correct one. This I do not believe he has done.

Let us violate the order which he follows and begin with *Ignotus.* If *Ignotus* is the correct interpretation, "these lines" must refer to the lines written upon the tombstones in the churchyard—and Professor Shepard admits that this is possible—but in making such an assumption the "advocate has done almost criminal violence to the phrase 'these lines'."[6] On the other hand, he feels it highly improbable that such a poet could have existed without "attracting some notice" or being mentioned in Gray's letters.[7] Hence he eliminates *Ignotus,* and I do not imagine that anyone is likely to object to that elimination.

Let us proceed to Gray himself. The chief support of this identi-

---

(New York: Harcourt, Brace, 1946), I, 914n. See also *English Prose and Poetry 1660–1800*. Odell Shepard, Paul Spencer Wood, eds. (New York: Houghton Mifflin, 1934), pp. 518–19, 1008, in which Professor Shepard's theory is explained in more detail.

[4] *Ibid.,* 913.

[5] Shepard, *MP,* 348.

[6] *Ibid.,* 349.

[7] *Ibid.*

fication "is found in the only easy and natural reading of the 24th stanza. Common sense insists, despite the pedantic objection of the *Ignotus* advocate, that 'these lines' must be the lines of the *Elegy* itself. . . ." [8] Yet the description of the youth does not fit Gray and would be in exceedingly bad taste; it is inconceivable that he would publish a portrait of himself containing such "lachrymose self-pity." [9] Most of this is perfectly reasonable. Gray almost certainly did not intend to give to the world, or even to only his friends, a picture of himself as an unappreciated youth dying of melancholy; but Professor Shepard seems to have overlooked a perfectly possible interpretation. If we assume that the person referred to is the author of the *Elegy*, must we necessarily regard that author as Thomas Gray, scholar, poet, and critic? May not the *Elegy* simply represent the musings of an unknown person, perhaps a village poet, rather than those of Thomas Gray himself? Surely such a poetic representation is far from unknown. Do we interpret the "I" that appears in works of literature written in the first person as invariably representing the author whose name appears on the cover? Are Roxana and Moll Flanders in reality Daniel Defoe? The thought is an arresting one. In any event, whether one accepts this interpretation or not is of little consequence, for it remains at least a possibility; and before Professor Shepard can eliminate "Thomas Gray," he must eliminate this—as he does not.

Poeta Professor Shepard objects to because he feels that it implies too abrupt a break in the change from generalized description to specific description: "A transition from this grandeur of generality to the consideration of an actual individual would be difficult to make and almost necessarily injurious to unity of total effect." [10] The "details in the description of the Youth and of his death are too minute for a conventionalized portrait," and "Gray could scarcely have expected that this highly romantic individual would be accepted by the public of 1750 as a typical poet." [11] Furthermore, such an interpretation would mean that there is "no sense for the 24th stanza" because there is no poetry to which "these lines" can refer: ". . . the difficulty here is to find any actual verses which may possibly be attributed to *Poeta*." Consequently, we "must conclude . . . that Gray had in mind some actual person. . . ." [12]

To all this, it seems to me, very grave objections may be raised. First, how is the transition from general remarks to a specific individual more harmful to the unity of the poem than what Professor

[8] *Ibid.*
[9] *Ibid.*, 350.
[10] *Ibid.*, 348.
[11] *Ibid.*
[12] *Ibid.*

Shepard thinks took place? Surely a transition from general musings
to an epitaph on Richard West is an even greater violation of unity.
Furthermore, if there is a flaw in the unity, surely that is an indication
of weak craftsmanship rather than proof that Gray was writing about
West. We shall discuss the details of the portrait a little later, but
one might mention here that the details, if the reader will re-examine
them, are actually somewhat vague. Certainly "minute" seems rather
an overstatement. Even more misleading is Professor Shepard's reference to a "conventionalized portrait." Why must this be regarded as a
conventionalized portrait? Passing over the somewhat sweeping nature
of the generalization that the public of 1750 could not be expected by
Gray to recognize this young man as a typical poet, we might reply
that there is no reason to believe Gray cared particularly what the
public thought. He certainly seems to show very few signs of ever
troubling himself about the opinions of most of his readers. It is
common knowledge that the publication of the *Elegy* was forced upon
him and that he felt little interest in explaining the *Odes* to the public:
"He despised the taste of the general reading public to such an extent
that he would publish nothing of his own accord. When the public
acclaimed the *Elegy,* he bore their approval with indifference; when
they criticized his Pindaric odes, he withdrew into his recluse's shell.
Sensitive to an extreme, he hated to offer his poems to the world." [13]
Under these conditions can we regard Professor Shepard's reference
to a "typical poet" as an adequate delineation of the possibilities?
Surely the point involved is that Gray is representing an unappreciated
young *village* poet—who surely would not be intended to represent
the "typical poet" of the eighteenth century! Furthermore, Professor
Shepard takes a little too much for granted when he assumes that
there is no poetry written by *Poeta* to which "these lines" may refer.
He admits reluctantly in the case of *Ignotus* that the phrase may mean
the "uncouth rimes" of l. 79, but why does he overlook the possibility
that they may be composed by *Poeta?* To be sure, he states in the
discussion of *Ignotus* that such an interpretation is "pedantic" and
does "criminal violence" to the normal reading of the poem, but this
is a palpable exaggeration, for surely the average intelligent reader
on observing that the "thee" does not refer to Gray, finds no difficulty
in assuming that the poem describes a fictitious village poet who had
commemorated the "unhonoured Dead."

Indeed, the restrictions with which Professor Shepard has surrounded
his three possibilities are not only too rigid but extremely misleading,
for they do not take into account what seems to me to be the obvious
meaning of the poem. Gray, I should imagine, begins his *Elegy* by
writing about a rather idealized churchyard and the rather idealized

[13] Jones, *Thomas Gray,* 146.

villagers who are its reluctant tenants. He does not necessarily have any particular spot in mind—in fact, the identification of the church-yard with Stoke Poges still seems to be debatable and for the purposes of this paper is of no importance. He then goes on to mention in some detail another example of unrewarded virtue, the village poet, who wrote the epitaphs. The young man is not a figure of any historical existence and he is not necessarily intended to be a typical poet or a conventionalized picture of a poet. Naturally he is melancholy: he never had an opportunity to win fame (just as the other villagers never did): he is a mute, inglorious Milton with all his noble rage repressed. All he can do is to write epitaphs for his defunct friends or relations, and it is no wonder melancholy marked him for her own. Under the same circumstances she would mark Professor Shepard for her own. Finally he dies, and an obliging versifier writes an epitaph for him.

Professor Shepard makes much of the facts that originally, according to Mason, the poem ended before the introduction of the Youth and that the "thou, who mindful of the unhonour'd Dead" of the first draft refers probably to Gray;[14] but if Gray simply decided to add a specific example of neglected genius in the form of a rustic poet to his poem, he quite naturally might feel that it was unnecessary to tamper any further with ll. 93–94, since they could easily be interpreted as a reference to the village poet. With a somewhat different application in mind, Professor Shepard comments: "Writing slowly and at long intervals, he may never . . . fully realize what flaws may lurk in its structure, what warpings past the aim." [15] And it seems to me that this is a much more probable explanation of the ambiguity of "thee" and "these lines" than the theory which Professor Shepard later ad-vances. However, Professor Shepard, after noting Mason's statement[16] that Gray had decided to give the poem a different conclusion, remarks that the rejected stanzas "are as good as any that he kept," [17] and that in its "original form . . . the 24th stanza was composed before the epitaph was attached to the poem." [18] Hence: ". . . the establishment of Mason's remark concerning the rejected stanzas, taken with our original hypothesis, indicates that at some time prior to June, 1750, Gray had among his papers two independent poems in the *Elegy* stanza: the epitaph, addressed to some person as yet unknown to us, and a poem in twenty-two stanzas about a country churchyard which ended with a clear reference to the poet himself." [19] Consequently, all

[14] Shepard, *MP*, 353–57.
[15] *Ibid.*, 357.
[16] *Ibid.*, 357n.
[17] *Ibid.*, 359.
[18] *Ibid.*, 360.
[19] *Ibid.*

the *Elegy* "from the 19th stanza to the Epitaph is really a sort of bridge thrown between these two preexisting piers." [20]

Now all this indicates nothing of the sort. In the first place, as I have attempted to point out, Professor Shepard has neither defined satisfactorily nor eliminated completely all of his three possibilities, and so weak a foundation necessarily renders unstable any structure which is raised upon it. But even had he succeeded, all this last reasoning indicates is that Gray decided to alter the conclusion of his poem so that he could add more to it. Certainly, he *may* have had two independent poems, but it is only a rare possibility, not an established conclusion, for it is at least equally possible that the "Epitaph" was written at a later date than were all the stanzas that now precede it.

Professor Shepard presents certain additional evidence to strengthen his argument that the section from the 19th stanza to the "Epitaph" is merely a bridge between two pre-existing poems, one of which is an epitaph for West. He quotes Mason's belief that the *Elegy* was probably begun in the summer of 1742 (and of course influenced by West's death): "I am inclined to believe that the *Elegy* . . . was begun if not concluded at this time also: though I am aware that as it stands at present the conclusion was of a later date." [21] Walpole, however, had not agreed with Mason. In a letter (December 1, 1773) he remarked that he had thought the *Elegy* was written three or four years after West's death. Mason apparently answered him in an unknown letter; and on December 14 Walpole replied: "Your account of the *Elegy* puts an end to my other criticism." [22] Professor Shepard comments: "What were the arguments by which Mason silenced Walpole's doubts[23] we can only surmise. It is probable, however, that they were in line with the reason which he implies in the *Memoirs* [see quotation from Mason above] for dating the poem 1742, connecting the poem with West's death still more closely than he cared to do in his book." [24] Gray, Professor Shepard believes, may have told Mason about the West family scandal,[25] and consequently Mason in his unknown letter to

[20] *Ibid.*

[21] *Ibid.*, 362. Quoted from Mason's *Memoirs of Gray*.

[22] *Ibid.*, 363.

[23] Walpole's doubts may not have been so completely silenced after all. In the definitive *Correspondence of Thomas Gray* edited by Toynbee and Whibley (Oxford, 1935, III, 1215) the editors remark: "Walpole was sometimes more polite than sincere in expressing agreement with his correspondents. . . ." In fact, they incline to believe that Mason was mistaken and that the poem was begun in 1746 (pp. 1214–16).

[24] Shepard, *MP*, 363–64.

[25] West is supposed to have suffered from the suspicion that his mother had carried on a liaison with her husband's secretary and perhaps had even poisoned her husband. See the Toynbee and Whibley *Correspondence*, I, 150–51, n. 3.

Walpole may have pointed out the "intimate connection of all this with the *Elegy*." [26]

All this theorizing is sheer guesswork. There is absolutely no evidence that I know of, save Professor Shepard's speculations, to prove that Mason was ever told by Gray the story of West's troubles; and, even if he had been, there is still no proof that this is what he wrote in his letter to Walpole. Furthermore, if such were the case, it still would not furnish conclusive proof that the *Elegy* was written in 1742. Finally whether the *Elegy* was written in 1742 or in 1750, we still do not have any assurance that the "Epitaph" was originally written for Richard West.

Another somewhat distressing note in this argument is Professor Shepard's fondness for the "sinister"—and unjustified—implication. He remarks: ". . . connecting the poem still more closely than he [Mason] cared to do in his book," and a little later he adds the following: "This view is in harmony with the testimony in favor of 1742 as the year in which the *Elegy* was begun, which testimony was given by a man who seems to have had better grounds for his assertion than any which *he finally saw fit* [my italics] to publish." [27] The implication of course is that Mason deliberately suppressed his reasons for believing the *Elegy* to have been begun in 1742 for fear of revealing the West scandal. Such an inference is without justification. Nowhere has Mason implied any such thing. In fact an even more probable inference is that his belief rested on nothing but a vague and unreliable recollection. In a very similar vein Professor Shepard discusses the hasty first publication of the *Elegy:* "In a very curious letter of Ash Wednesday, 1751, he [Gray] thanks Walpole for the 'great decency' with which he has managed this 'little misfortune'. . . ." [28] Professor Shepard regards the matter with a suspicious eye: "This fear of printer's ink seems something more than a late example of gentlemanly reluctance to professed authorship." [29] We of course are supposed to assume from this that Gray was horrified at the thought of having a poem connected with West put in print—another completely unsupported inference, for just what is "curious" about this letter? Nothing that I can find, for as may be easily seen in an examination of it,[30] the general tone of the letter is mildly flippant. Indeed there is no indication whatsoever of "something more" than a gentlemanly aversion to publication, since we already know that Gray was chronically unenthusiastic about such matters. Implications of this sort can

[26] Shepard, *MP*, 364–65.
[27] *Ibid.*, 372.
[28] *Ibid.*, 368.
[29] *Ibid.*, 368–69.
[30] Toynbee and Whibley, *Correspondence*, I, 342–43.

only serve to increase our doubts of Professor Shepard's entire hypothesis.

Professor Shepard's final step is to examine the description of the Youth and to point out its resemblance to Richard West.[31] He explains that West was Gray's dearest friend, solitary, crazed with care, and a poet cut short in his prime. Science did not frown upon him, for he was supposed "to have been more learned than Gray." [32] It is true that he was not of humble birth ("he was a grandson of Bishop Burnet and son of a vice-chancellor of Ireland" [33]), but the phrase "gives no more trouble in interpreting the Epitaph with reference to West than it does when considering the Epitaph as written by Gray for himself." [34] Finally the Youth is described by a line very similar to the one West used about himself ("A Muse as yet unheeded and unknown," *Monody on the Death of Queen Caroline*).[35]

Now one obvious flaw in this chain of reasoning is that the only alternative is not Thomas Gray himself, for the description will fit both the rustic poet and a poet (not necessarily Gray) whose musings are embodied in the *Elegy* better than it will fit either Gray or West. Certainly the line "A Youth to Fortune and to Fame unknown" may indeed be an echo of West's line, for it very probably would unconsciously—or consciously—come into Gray's mind when describing a talented, melancholy youth who died before he achieved recognition; but such an echo certainly cannot be regarded as proof that Gray was deliberately using the line to describe West.

Let us examine this description of the Youth in regard to its application to West. To me it seems far too hazy to have much significance. In the first place, the village poet would be even more likely to wander about the countryside than West would, and he surely would be cut short in his prime, since such a demise would give Gray a most convenient way to end a graveyard poem concerned with unrewarded virtue. Second, West did indeed have a friend; but so have a good many other million men. Furthermore, the reader will observe that "friend" rimes very satisfactorily with "send" and poets have been known to be influenced by such considerations. Third, "humble birth" is rather difficult, as Professor Shepard seems to realize, to account for in a poem which was originally written to commemorate the son of a vice-chancellor and the grandson of a Bishop, but it is the obvious phrase to employ in the description of a village poet. Fourth, "Fair Science frowned not on his humble birth"—if we ignore the "humble

[31] Shepard, *MP*, 369–71.
[32] *Ibid.*, 371.
[33] *Ibid.*
[34] *Ibid.*
[35] *Ibid.*, 370.

birth"—might apply to West, but it is equally suitable as a description of an imaginary rustic poet who had a certain amount of talent and knowledge. Surely on the basis of so hazy a line as this we are not justified in assigning the description to West!

Of course one may attempt to answer my objections by pointing out that although each of Professor Shepard's arguments is trifling and easily explained away, the mere accumulation is significant. I cannot quite follow this logic myself, but even if we grant the point, such an accumulation would be of value only if the "Epitaph" alone existed or if we *knew* that it once had had an independent existence and if we, naturally, were then searching among Gray's friends for its subject. But such I believe I have demonstrated is not the case. The obvious person, I repeat, is merely a young rustic versifier, a poetic ideal of a sort, and the description applies to him more convincingly than it does to West. Hence how can we regard Professor Shepard's conclusion as even probable, much less proved?

There is, of course, no proof that Professor Shepard's theory is not correct. It is perfectly possible that it accurately represents the truth, but it seems to me that these are several further objections that must be answered before this conjecture can be accepted as more than a bare possibility.

1. There is absolutely no known manuscript or reference in any correspondence relating to Gray that would clearly indicate the existence of the "Epitaph" as a separate poem. Again this does not prove that such a situation did not exist, but in any reasonable weighing of evidence this point is not one that can be as completely ignored as Professor Shepard ignores it.

2. Walpole also was an intimate friend of West. Is it not rather odd that if the "Epitaph" refers to West, there is no comment on that matter in the existing—and most of it does exist—Walpole-Gray correspondence? Even though the two men were estranged for a few years, they still would be likely to mention the subject when their friendship was resumed, especially since Walpole was so closely connected with the publication of the *Elegy*.

3. Furthermore, even if the "Epitaph" did refer to West, why on earth should Gray, or Walpole, or Mason seek to suppress that fact? Why should there be this frenzy of delicacy that Professor Shepard seems to think existed? Certainly not because of any family scandal. The most suspicious of readers could hardly derive from the lines "And Melancholy marked him for her own" and "He gave to Misery all he had, a tear" the fact that West suspected his mother of conducting a liaison and of poisoning his father.

4. In fact, why did not Gray openly acknowledge the "Epitaph" as a separate poem mourning the loss of his friend instead of incor-

porating it in disguise in another poem? Not from sheer bashfulness, for he had not hesitated to write his famous sonnet to West.

In conclusion, I might say that had Professor Shepard contented himself with advancing as a mere possibility his theory that the "Epitaph" was originally written as a separate poem lamenting the death of West, I should have no objections. The idea is an interesting and stimulating one. But, unfortunately, he does not pause at this point. He remarks: "A hypothesis has met its supreme test when it solves not only the problem which it was designed to cover but also the cognate problems that arise during further investigation." [36] And: "We may safely say, then, that the hypothesis with which we began has justified itself, and that it has led to this sound conclusion: *aut West, aut Diabolus*." [37] When such positive statements as this are made and when they are repeated as well grounded in undergraduate textbooks it seems to me time to protest that Professor Shepard has merely advanced a tissue of guesswork, which, like many similar tissues, cannot be positively disproved, but which in no sense of the word can be regarded as proved.

[36] *Ibid.*, 372.
[37] *Ibid.*

Gray's *Elegy*: The Biographical Problem
in Literary Criticism

by Frank H. Ellis

It is a problem in literary criticism to know how to use the growing store of material discovered by historical research. This is only the practical aspect of a larger, theoretical problem: the relation between a written work and the biographical experiences of the writer. It has never been doubted that a poet's experiences, public and private, historical and psychological, reappear, distorted, refined, generalized, reordered, in his poetry. Hence it follows that the reconstruction of the poet's experiences from diaries, letters, accounts of friends, and public records, may illuminate his poetry. But the converse of this proposition is also assumed to be true: if the biographical experience illuminates the poetry, the poetry must also illuminate the biographical experience. The poem, in other words, is an autobiographical document.

The argument of this essay is intended to show that the latter conclusion is false and that biographical experiences can no more be reconstructed from a poem than the poem (if it were lost) could be reconstructed from the experiences. The argument is concerned, however, with critical rather than biographical problems. Formal biography based on this fallacy is easily recognized as a variety of historical fiction. But formal criticism based on the biographical fallacy (as it may be called) can be positively misleading.

Gray's *Elegy* is chosen as the vehicle for this argument because it has long been censured for its intrusive autobiographical detail. And this complaint has been made not only by writers who were Gray's contemporaries but by such recent critics as William Empson and Cleanth Brooks, who are ordinarily chary of introducing biographical considerations into literary criticism. The choice of the *Elegy* was also made because adverse criticism of a purely formal nature, namely that

the poem lacks a coherent structure, can so clearly be shown to rest
on the assumption that the poem is excessively autobiographical. What
seems necessary, therefore, is a determination of the extent to which
Gray's experiences actually figure in the poem. Then the problem of
the poem's structure may be resumed without prejudice. For so long
as it is assumed that the poet's rôle is of one sort, it is impossible to
discover any structural pattern that assigns to him another part.

[Ellis explains that, as we can tell from Gray's letters, the poet
was in London during the trial of those Scottish noblemen who had
supported Charles Stuart during the rebellion of 1745 (see essay by
Newman, pp. 17ff.). Ellis quotes the elaborately formal details of the
grand procession before the trial, which Gray attended on two days
and described in a letter to Wharton. Gray also spent several days
at various impressive public events, and these events are reflected
in the *Elegy*. Also Gray visited Walpole at Windsor, where he saw
the Duke of Cumberland with his mistresses and attendants. He reflected on the rebel Lord Balmerino's composure at his trial and
must have considered the philosophic implications involved when one
rejected fame and grandeur. Ellis quotes the last four stanzas of the
first draft of the *Elegy* (see Introduction, p. 8) and Gray's 1750 letter
in which he tells Walpole that he has at last added an "end" to a
poem the beginning of which Walpole had seen long before. In this
first draft (the Eton MS), Gray, like Milton in *Lycidas,* was really
writing about himself.]

It is evident from this that Gray's experience in reading *Lycidas* was
of equal importance in the composition of the *Elegy* with the varied
experiences of the holiday in London and Stoke Poges. That Gray read
Lycidas (and a score of other poems) may be deduced from the *Elegy*
itself. But nothing else of Gray's public or private experiences could
be inferred from the *Stanza's* in the absence of external documents. It
could never be guessed that "No more with Reason & thyself at Strife"
means that Gray disappointed his parents by not pursuing a career at
law. Nor could it ever be deduced from "The thoughtless World to
Majesty may bow" that Gray encountered the Duke of Cumberland
at the Windsor races. All that might be deduced from the original
Stanza's is that the author once felt somewhat frustrated and neglected.
But this would be meaningless since it could be assumed to be true
of every poet at some moment.

Perhaps it was because the conclusion of the *Stanza's* was so earnest
that Gray did not show it to Walpole. In letters to his friend, Gray assumed quite a different tone: he affected the pose of the gentleman
amateur of the arts. It would not do to let Walpole know how seriously
he regarded his art. The cult of the *amateur* demanded carelessness,
and impersonality, and wit. Later this pose forced Gray to profess

shame at seeing his name in print, to insist that it be preceded by *Mr.* on the title page of his poems. He scorned to be thought "a mere poet." Perhaps this was not wholly a pose. Gray never threw off "the Pruderie & Reserve of a Cambridge Student" which he himself observed as an undergraduate. A later Cambridge graduate did, of course, and was thereby enabled to write a 7,881-line *Prelude, Or, Growth of a Poet's Mind, An Autobiographical Poem.* But Gray was not so self-indulgent. He had a real fear of appearing ridiculous and of revealing the content of his mind (except through the medium of dramatic *personae*). His modesty was not a pose. Thomas Gray's "poetic" autobiography is contained in twenty words which he wrote to Walpole near the end of his life: "whenever the humour takes me," he said, "I will write, because I like it; and because I like myself better when I do so." [1] And even as he wrote these words to a lifelong friend, Gray recognized that he was being preternaturally "candid."

At any rate, in his revision of the *Stanza's,* what Gray did was to depersonalize them entirely. He struck out the "y" in "thy," wrote "eir" instead, and thus completely altered the reference and intention of the poem. If it was really to be the "artless Tale" of "the unhonour'd Dead," however, a totally different conclusion would have to be written for it, a conclusion which shifted the bearing of the poem from the Poet to the rustics. This is exactly what Gray did. He cancelled the intensely personal four-stanza conclusion and refocussed the poem on "the Poor":

> Far from the madding Crowd's ignoble Strife;
> *Their* sober Wishes never knew to stray:
> Along the cool sequester'd Vale of Life
> *They* kept the silent Tenour of *their* Way,

which is a remarkably economical revision of the original concluding stanza: [see "No more with Reason. . . .", Introduction, p. 8, ll. 85ff.]. Then, in the sixteen additional stanzas which he added in the manuscript, Gray created a dramatic situation involving four characters.

This situation simply develops an idea implicit in "The short & simple Annals of the Poor." In the original draft of the *Stanza's* there was no description of the tombstones in the village churchyard. The graves were mentioned in the fourth stanza, but there was no explicit description of the grave-markers to contrast with the description of the mortuary sculpture which marked the tombs of the rich, the "Trophies . . . storied Urn . . . animated Bust." There was, however, an implicit reference to the humble tombstones in "The short & simple Annals." For the historical "Annals" of the poor reduce to two: Born

---

[1] *Correspondence of Thomas Gray,* ed., Paget Toynbee and Leonard Whibley (Oxford, 1935), III, 1018.

16—, Died 17—. And this suggests the simple notation of vital statistics which appears on churchyard markers. It was to the latter, therefore, that Gray turned his attention in the next two stanzas which he added to the poem:

> Yet even these Bones from Insult to protect
> Some frail Memorial still erected nigh
> With uncouth Rhime, & shapeless Sculpture deckt
> Implores the passing Tribute of a Sigh.
>
> Their Names, their Years [cf. "Annals"], spelt by th' unletter'd Muse
> The Place of Fame, & Epitaph supply
> And many a holy Text around she strews,
> That teach the rustic moralist to die.

The existence of the rustic markers presupposes the existence of a rustic artist, who chisels into the soft stone the name and dates of birth and death and who composes some "uncouth Rhime" or chooses some "Text" from the Bible to decorate the grave-marker. Among peasants whom Gray had already described as illiterate, there must now be imagined some semi-literate artisan on whom the village could rely to frame "Some frail Memorial":

> For who to dumb Forgetfulness, a Prey
> This pleasing anxious Being e'er resign'd;
> Left the warm Precincts of the chearful Day,
> Nor cast one longing lingring Look behind?
>
> On *some fond Breast* the parting Soul relies,
> Some pious Drops the closing Eye requires;
> Even from the Tomb the Voice of Nature cries,
> And buried Ashes glow with Social Fires.

But who was there among the illiterate peasantry on whom the rustic artist himself could rely for a similar office? Who, in short, would write the epitaph-writer's epitaph?

Gray assigns this rôle to a literate outlander, the Spokesman of the poem, the "me" of line 4. But in order to introduce the "Epitaph" into the poem, a further dramatic complication had to be invented. Gray imagines that after the village Stonecutter is dead and buried, another melancholy wayfarer ("Some kindred Spirit") will enter the churchyard seeking to learn of the Stonecutter's fate. Still another peasant ("some hoary-headed Swain") will be able to tell the Enquirer something of the irregular life of the Stonecutter and point to the "Epitaph" written by the Spokesman and now fixed over the Stonecutter's grave.

Here was a chance for Gray to salvage another of the four cancelled stanzas. He first planned *two* stanzas introducing the Enquirer:

> For Thee, who mindful &c: as above.

> If chance that e'er some pensive Spirit more,
> By sympathetic Musings here delay'd,
> With vain tho' kind, Enquiry shall explore
> Thy once-loved Haunt, this long-deserted Shade.

The "as above," of course, refers to the rejected stanza: [See "And thou . . . .", Introduction, p. 8, ll. 77–80] where "thou" was clearly a personal reference to Gray himself. But then, in a subsequent revision, Gray combined these two stanzas into one:

> For Thee, who mindful of th'unhonour'd Dead
> Dost in these Lines their artless Tale relate,
> If chance by lonely Contemplation led
> Some kindred Spirit shall enquire thy Fate,

where "Thee" refers to the Stonecutter, not to Gray, "these Lines" to the "uncouth Rhimes" composed by the Stonecutter, not to *Stanza's wrote in a country church-yard,* and "Some kindred Spirit" to the chance Enquirer. By a shift in the antecedent of a pronoun, Gray wrote himself out of his poem.

In the words which the aged Swain speaks in response to the Enquirer, the character of the Stonecutter is revealed to be that of the conventional pastoral poet. Then, in two more stanzas, the Swain describes the death of the Stonecutter and points out his tombstone, where the literate Enquirer may read the "Epitaph." This drastic revision of the poem, which made it twice as long as the original *Stanza's,* satisfies all the imagined requirements. The epitaph-writer's epitaph affords a nice "Turn" of wit which contrasts sharply with the earnest protestations of the original conclusion. Shifting the reference of the poem from the Poet to the peasants and the peasant-poet fully satisfies the requirement of impersonality. The vague "me" of the first stanza refers no longer to Gray but to a completely generalized Spokesman who is simply the vehicle of the poem. "For thee," in line 93, introduces the Spokesman's apostrophe to the Stonecutter, not Gray's apostrophe to himself, and the "Friend" in the next-to-the-last stanza must represent the "kindred Spirit" who comes to enquire for the Stonecutter and learns he is dead.

Here, then, is a poem which achieves total "anonymity" despite its subjective genesis. And here, at last, is a *"thing with an end"* which Gray could show to Walpole, and which Walpole could not help showing about until it fell into the uncircumcized hands of the proprietor of the *Magazine of Magazines. Lycidas,* however, remained the model even for this wholesale revision of the poem. The idea for the Stonecutter's epitaph would seem to have been supplied by *Lycidas* 19–22, where the poet who was constrained to sing for Lycidas is reconciled to his task by the hope that a similar "melodious Tear" will be shed at his death:

> So may som gentle Muse
> With lucky words favour my destin'd Urn,
> And as he passes turn,
> And bid fair peace be to my sable shrowd.

Gray acknowledges the obligation: "Some pious Drops the closing Eye requires." It is as if in fulfillment of Milton's hope that Gray includes the "Epitaph" for the Stonecutter's "destin'd Urn." The Stonecutter is not Milton, of course, but he may have been a "mute inglorious Milton," and he was, in a sense, a poet. The writer of "uncouth Rhimes" in the *Elegy,* who sheds "a Tear" for "th'unhonour'd Dead" has something in common even with the "uncouth Swain" in *Lycidas* who sheds a "melodious tear" for the "Unwept" shepherd. And the "consolation" which is offered to the "unknown" rustic is strangely like the "consolation" of Phoebus Apollo:

> *Elegy,* 125–28:
>
> No farther seek his Merits to disclose
> Nor seek to draw them from their dread Abode
> (His frailties there in trembling Hope repose)
> The Bosom of his Father & and his God.

> *Lycidas,* 81–84:
>
> [*Fame*] lives and spreds aloft by those pure eyes,
> And perfet witness of all-judging *Jove;*
> As he pronounces lastly on each deed,
> Of so much fame in Heav'n expect thy meed.

In the original *Stanza's,* the narrator, with whom Gray identified himself, occupied the central position of the "uncouth Swain" who mourns for Lycidas. But in the completed *Elegy,* the Spokesman is relegated to the position of the anonymous elegist whom the "uncouth Swain" in *Lycidas* momentarily invokes, and the central position is occupied by the village Stonecutter who mourns "th'unhonour'd Dead." Gray has shifted the bearing of the poem from the conflict of the Poet with an alien world to the triumphant persistence, or continuity, of poetry, despite this hostile world. And this is what may be implied in the concluding line of *Lycidas:* "To morrow to fresh Woods, and Pastures new." [For Gray's annoyance at learning the *Magazine of Magazines* planned to publish the *Elegy* and his letter to Walpole arranging for Dodsley's printing of the poem, see Introduction, p. 9. Ellis discusses eighteenth-century admiration of the clarity of the poem as contrasted with Romantic opinions that it was confused, and proceeds to review the later criticism, which usually assumes the reference in l. 93 is to the poet himself.]

Taken altogether, the bulk of this writing is interesting mainly because it testifies to the persisting vitality of the *Elegy,* but incidentally because it illustrates some of the more persistent fallacies in literary criticism. The first of these is the biographical fallacy, the assumption that an exact, one-to-one correspondence exists between the person who is imagined to be speaking the lines of a poem (the Spokesman) and the historical personage who is known to have written the poem.

A simple form of this error occurs in the first critical review of the *Elegy,* which appeared in a column called "The Inspector" written by John Hill for the *London Daily Advertiser, and Literary Gazette* of 5 March 1751. Some of Hill's criticism is perceptive and acute. Despite the fact that he apparently did not know who wrote it, he boldly proclaimed the *Elegy* "One of the best poems the present age has produced" and he noticed immediately a "striking Likeness" between the *Elegy* and *Lycidas.* With equal but unwarranted boldness he assumed that "the author" and the person who is imagined to be speaking the lines of the poem are indistinguishable. Hill was certain that "the author" is present on the scene which is described in the poem, but he could not decide exactly where he is. In one place he wrote, "The author introduces himself walking over the graves of the deceased humble villagers, in a melancholy and contemplative humour." But in the second paragraph following he flatly contradicted himself: "Let us recollect the situation of the poet, in a still evening, contemplating, from an elevated spot, the country round him, while there is scarce light for the prospect." In the first instance the critic was obviously thinking of lines 13–16:

> Beneath those rugged Elms, that Yewtree's Shade,
> Where heaves the Turf in many a mould'ring Heap,
> Each in his narrow Cell for ever laid,
> The rude Forefathers of the Hamlet sleep,

and in the second instance he was thinking of the familiar opening stanzas of the poem.

The person whom Gray imagines to be speaking the lines of the poem is indeed "contemplating . . . the country round him" in the opening lines. But there is no indication that he is looking down from "an elevated spot." Nor is there any evidence that he later walks over the graves in the churchyard. Except for one word, "me," and the presence which disturbs the "mopeing Owl," there is no indication of the Spokesman's existence, much less of his exact "situation" or movements. There is even very little that can be inferred from the poem about his character. He obviously derives from a social class and milieu different from that of the "rude" peasants whom he describes. It is evident that he has not been denied "Knowledge . . . Rich with the Spoils of Time" for he is able to make graceful allusion to Dante and Petrarch. He seems to be a gentleman, but his attitude toward gentility implies disenchantment; he has "known them all already, known them all": the mockery of Ambition, the disdainful smile of Grandeur, the provocations of Honour, the blandishments of Flattery. His very presence in the graveyard, so far from "the *madding* Crowd's *ignoble* Strife," implies dissatisfaction with his own class and milieu. And his scorn of bourgeois art, which heaps "the Shrine of Luxury and Pride/With Incense kindled at the Muse's Flame," supplies further evidence that the Spokesman is a kind of *déclassé* intellectual. Any similarity he may bear to the historical figure, Thomas Gray, is not, of course, purely coincidental, but simply irrelevant to the purposes of the poem. For he is mentioned in line 4 and then is made to serve no function in the poem except that of narrator, and composer of the "Epitaph."

What is actually presented in the opening stanzas is a series of images establishing the time, place, and tone of the poem. The *passage* of time is also very carefully noted. In lines 4–6 the last streaks of light fade from the sky and by line 10 the moon has risen. The poem opens with an auditory image, "The Curfeu . . . ." This is followed by one image which is both auditory and visual, "The lowing Herd . . . ," and by another which is both visual and kinesthetic, "The Plowman homeward plods his weary Way." Besides the explicit references in lines 4–6, the fading of light is further implied by two effects in the next lines: images of sound now outnumber images of sight, and the sounds themselves, the droning of a beetle, the tinkling of distant wetherbells, and the hooting of an owl, produce a *decrescendo* from the original tolling of bells and lowing of cattle. In the moonlight the visual images reduce to the objects of the immediate scene: the black mass of an "ivy-mantled Tower" and the turf-grown graves. Even in the moonlit scene it comes as something of a shock to learn that these graves lie beneath a "Yewtree's *Shade*."

There may be no image here at all, but simply a metaphor. Gray may be using the word "Shade" in a figurative sense of "shelter" or "canopy," in which case the choice of "Shade," with its connotation of ghosts and spirits, would be a pregnant one. But there seems to be at least an equal probability that the "Yewtree's Shade" represents a momentary failure in Gray's imagination of the scene. Gray is describing a scene, partly from the memory of specific churchyards, no doubt, but mainly from imagination and convention, the memory of specific literary descriptions. It has long been recognized that the poem is a *cento* of quotation and allusion, and Gray acknowledged the existence (if not the extent) of this aspect of the poem when he added notes to the *Elegy* in the first collected edition of his poems in 1768, indicating, for example, that "The Curfeu tolls the Knell of parting Day" is imitated from Dante's "squilla di lontano/che paia il giorno pianger che si more." No "source" has yet been suggested for the commonplace "Yewtree's Shade," but it is not unlikely that one exists. Even the periphrasis "narrow Cell," in the same stanza, has an exact correlative in Horace's "angustis . . . cellis" (*Satires* 1, vii. 8) which appears in a passage describing the graves of "the Poor." So Gray may have had in mind some such line as "Beneath the gloomy Covert of an Yew," from *The Dispensary,* or "Under the shade of melancholy boughs," in *As You Like It,* when he wrote "Beneath . . . that Yew-tree's Shade."

Whatever its origins, this phrase may serve to recall the supposition that Gray was in London when he began the *Elegy*. And in any case, "the author" could not possibly have been present on the scene described in the poem. For this scene is literary, not topographical. The churchyard is not Stoke Poges, which was by no means a "neglected Spot," was barely within sound of the Windsor Castle bells, had only an inconspicuous tower, and probably no yewtrees. Nor is it Upton near Slough, nor Grantchester, nor Madingley, nor Thanington. This churchyard has no local habitation and no name. It is made up wholly of poetic images. Gray would not have included a "Yewtree's Shade" in this series of images if he had been describing a scene from sight. But he was constructing a scene from imagination, and apparently, in this line, he was imagining the graves as they might appear in daylight. (The next stanza begins with "The breezy Call of . . . *Morn.*") But whether or not it is to be interpreted as a failure, the "Yewtree's Shade" has served its present purpose if it has effected a sharp cleavage between "the author" at his writing table and the anonymous person who is imagined to be speaking the lines of the poem in some dim churchyard of the mind.

This "person" is as much a creature of Gray's imagination as Caliban is of Shakespeare's. And there is no more warrant for confusing the creature with the creator in one case than in the other. There might have been some warrant for confusing Gray and the Spokesman of the original *Stanza's,* but even in this case the Spokesman was an obviously conventional character of the species *poeta ignotus.* And Gray's wholesale revision of the poem completely dissociated himself from this character. This circumstance makes the *Elegy* an outstanding example for the study of the biographical fallacy which identifies literary creature and creator. And it is the biographical fallacy which underlies some of the more extravagant criticism of the *Elegy*.

It is only a step, for example, from the assumption that "the author" is present on the scene described in the poem to the further assumption that the poem was actually written in a churchyard. This step was first taken in an anonymous pamphlet, *A Criticism on the Elegy*, which has been attributed to one John Young.[2] [Ellis discusses how Young assumed the *Elegy* was actually written in a churchyard, and how David Cecil in *Two Quiet Lives* narrowed the churchyard down to Stoke Poges, the date to August 1742, and Gray's thoughts to West.]

In the second of the stanzas which Gray added in the revision, the poem was brought back, for the first time since the opening stanzas, to the scene in the churchyard, to consider now the rude tombstones. On these stones are recorded "The short and simple Annals of the Poor" —"Their Name, their Years, *spelt by th'unletter'd Muse*"—which one editor of the *Elegy* glosses as "composed or engraved by an illiterate *person*." It might be more plausible to read "composed or engraved by a semi-literate person inspired by the unnamed Muse of primitive art," for the gravestones are embellished with "uncouth Rhimes and shapeless Sculpture." The crux of the matter, however, lies in the recognition of this "person." His existence is further required by lines 89–90:

> On some fond Breast the parting Soul relies,
> Some pious Drops the closing Eye requires.

For it is the Stonecutter, not "the author" or even the Spokesman of the poem, who "gave to Mis'ry all he had, a Tear." The Spokesman is merely paying "The passing Tribute of a Sigh." It is the Stonecutter on whom the villagers rely for a more substantial and enduring tribute, some "Memorial" to supply "The Place of Fame and Elegy." It is the Stonecutter whose tears figuratively engrave the tombstones with "uncouth Rhimes and shapeless Sculpture." And finally, therefore, it must be the Stonecutter who is apostrophized by the Spokesman in lines 93–97:

> For *thee,* who mindful of th'unhonour'd Dead
> Dost in these Lines [cf. "uncouth Rhimes"] their artless Tale relate;
> If chance, by lonely Contemplation led,
> Some kindred Spirit shall inquire *thy* Fate,
> Haply some hoary-headed Swain may say, &c.

Hill, on the other hand, assumed that what follows in the poem is the author's "account of himself, when dead." So inevitably he was led to

[2] *A Criticism on the Elegy written in a Country Church Yard. Being a Continuation of Dr. J——n's Criticism on the Poems of Gray* (London, 1783). . . .

conclude that the "Epitaph" is Thomas Gray's epitaph. He quoted the second stanza of the "Epitaph" with this comment: "In fine, his character of himself, his expectations, and his content, are at once justly, greatly, and pleasingly expressed," which might be appropriate if the "Epitaph" were assumed to celebrate the death of an "unknown" village poet, but is simply mawkish if the "Epitaph" is made to represent Thomas Gray shedding a "pious" tear for himself.[3]

Yet this assumption has been made by virtually every critic of the *Elegy*.[4] Particularly after the publication of Mason's *Memoirs* in 1775 it became even more tempting to make elaborate conflations of Gray's private life with the Stonecutter's imagined existence. John Langhorne, in his review of Mason's *Memoirs*, was the first to remark the similarity between Gray's letter to Walpole from Burnham Beeches and the ancient Swain's account of the Stonecutter. Here is the letter, in part:

> [Burnham Beeches] is a little Chaos of Mountains & Precipices . . . just such hills as people, who love their Necks as well as I do, may venture to climb, & Crags, that give the eye as much pleasure, as if they were more dangerous: both Vale & Hill is cover'd over with most venerable Beeches, & other very reverend Vegetables, that like most ancient People, are always dreaming out their Stories to the Winds
>
> > And, as they bow their hoary Tops, relate
> > In murm'ring Sounds the dark Decrees of Fate;
> > While Visions, as Poetic eyes avow,
> > Cling to each Leaf, & swarm on ev'ry Bough:
>
> At the foot of one of these squats me I; il Penseroso, and there grow to the Trunk for a whole morning,
>
> > —the tim'rous Hare, & Sportive Squirrel
> > Gambol around me—
>
> like Adam in Paradise, but commonly without an Eve, & besides I think he did not use to read Virgil, as I usually do there: in this situation I often converse with my Horace aloud too, that is, talk to you; for I don't remember, that I ever heard you answer me.

[3] Cf. Lord David Cecil, "The Poetry of Thomas Gray," *Warton Lecture on English Poetry* (London, 1945), p. 11: "This brings Gray around to himself. How does he expect to be remembered? Not as a happy man: he has been sad, obscure, misunderstood. Yet, he reminds himself with his customary balance, there have been alleviations. He has known friendship, loved learning, and attained, in part at least, to virtue."

[4] Two exceptions are J. Crofts, *Gray: Poetry and Prose* (Oxford, 1926), p. vi, and Herbert W. Starr, " 'A Youth to Fortune and to Fame Unknown': a Re-estimation," [pp. 41ff.]. Crofts simply mentions without any elaboration "the hypothetical epitaph of a hypothetical youth." Starr, in an excellent rejoinder to Odell Shepard's repeated assurances that the *Epitaph* celebrates Richard West, develops at some length his contention that it celebrates "an imaginary rustic poet."

From this Langhorne draws the expected conclusion: Gray's "squatting
at the foot of one of the venerable beaches, and his growing to the
trunk for a whole morning, together with his conversation with himself, are faithfully drawn in his own poetical picture," [5] and goes on to
quote the Swain's words:

> 'Oft have we seen him at the Peep of Dawn
> 'Brushing with hasty Steps the Dews away
> 'To meet the Sun upon the upland Lawn.
>   'There at the Foot of yonder nodding Beech
> 'That wreathes its old fantastic Roots so high,
> 'His listless Length at Noontide would he stretch
> 'And pore upon the Brook that babbles by.
>   'Hard by yon Wood, now frowning as in Scorn,
> 'Mutt'ring his wayward Fancies he would rove,
> 'Now drooping, woeful wan, like one forlorn.
> 'Or craz'd with Care, or cross'd in hopeless Love.'

This would almost seem to prove that the biographical fallacy is not
fallacious at all. Gray *must* be describing himself in the poem because
he described himself in a similar situation in a letter written ten years
before the poem was begun. The "origin" of this passage in the *Elegy*,
as Langhorne concludes, *must* lie in Gray's activities during the
summer of 1736.

Actually, however, this passage has quite different origins. It was
mentioned before that the character of the Stonecutter is purely conventional, but it remains to document this fact. In the first place, two
phrases in the first three lines of the aged Swain's account connect the
Stonecutter with *Lycidas*. "Peep of Dawn" and "upland Lawn" recall

> Together both, ere the high Lawns appear'd
> Under the opening eye-lids of the morn,
> We drove a field. . . .

The next stanza is imitated very closely from the account of "melancholy Jaques":

>   he lay along
> Under an oak, whose antique root peep'd out
> Upon a brook, that brawls along this wood.

(Milton's melancholy man, too, would hide for hours "in close covert
by som Brook.") The Stonecutter's secret grief bears some affinity to
Spenser's Colin Cloute,

[5] *The Monthly Review: or, Literary Journal,* LII (May, 1775), 380. For the
ascription of this article to John Langhorne, see Benjamin Christie Nangle, *The
Monthly Review . . . Indexes of Contributors and Articles* (Oxford, 1934), pp. 26,
116.

> For pale and wanne he was, (alas the while,)
> May seeme he lovd, or els some care he tooke.

And the whole passage describing the Stonecutter's behavior recalls Vergil's second *Eclogue:*

> Formosum pastor Corydon ardebat Alexim,
> delicias domini, nec, quid speraret, habebat.
> tantum inter densas, umbrosa cacumina, fagos
> .adsidue veniebat. ibi haec incondita solus
> montibus et silvis studio iactabat inani.[6]

The similarity which Langhorne discovered between Gray's letter and the lines in the *Elegy* may be explained by the supposition that both are derived from this passage in Vergil. Gray mentioned that he had been reading Vergil and it seems that what he is doing in the letter is playing Corydon, frequenting the places where the high beeches ("most venerable Beeches") cast a dark shade, complaining aloud of his love for Alexis ("my Horace") to the woods and mountains ("both Vale & Hill") in rude fragments of verse ("And, as they bow their hoary Tops, relate/In murm'ring Sounds . . ." &c.). The similarity exists because for a moment during the long holiday from Cambridge Gray pretended to be the conventional lovelorn swain which he later represented the Stonecutter to be in the *Elegy*. The relationship between the episode from Gray's biography and the episode from the Stonecutter's imaginary life is not causal, but genetic. Both are derived from a common source, a literary convention. The Stonecutter is not Thomas Gray; he is Corydon *cum* Colin Cloute *cum* Jaques *cum* Lycidas. Thomas Gray, in an access of undergraduate spirits, once imagined himself to be a melancholy Corydon.[7] Sometimes Nature mimics Art. This is the only likely connection between Gray's letter and the lines in the *Elegy*.

Lord David Cecil, however, interprets the matter in a different light. He converts the Stonecutter's conventional behavior into biographical data and reasons backward from the poem to Gray's own experience: "he would loiter along, smiling ['now smiling as in Scorn'], frowning, murmuring aloud to himself ['Mutt'ring his wayward Fancies'], and then suddenly flinging down, to lie for hours beneath the shadow of oak or beech tree ['yonder nodding Beech']." [8] But not even the letter

---

[6] [The shepherd Corydon burned with passion for the handsome Alexis, the darling of his master, and did not know what to hope for. All he could do was to keep going constantly to the shady peaks, amidst thick beech trees. There, all alone, with vain longing he used to put forth these rude verses to the hills and forests.]

[7] Later in the same year Gray wrote to Walpole in a similar vein: "if I cannot die like a Hero, let it at least be like a despairing lover" (*Correspondence of Gray,* 1, 54).

[8] *Two Quiet Lives,* p. 130.

from Burnham Beeches requires the biographer to assume that Gray actually behaved in the wholly conventional manner described here, particularly a letter written in an age which talked about "the epistolary art." Everyone assumes some sort of attitude in writing a letter. And when this attitude becomes a conscious pose, the literalness of the experience described needs to be sharply discounted.

Yet this letter continued to be quoted to support the assumption that the person described by the ancient Swain was the historical personage, Thomas Gray. John Young, or pseudo-Johnson (as the author of *A Criticism on the Elegy* more properly might be called), was certain that Gray is describing himself in the last dozen stanzas of the poem because, as he said, "The beech seems *literally* to have been Gray's 'favourite Tree'." He found it fantastic that Gray should allude to his own death "and even . . . the epitaph on his stone" but he did not find it fantastic that a man who is imagined to be dead and buried should write a poem.

On the assumption that Gray is actually presenting an "account of himself, when dead," a number of critics have found fault with the latter part of the *Elegy* and with the "Epitaph" in particular. Odell Shepard thought it "scarcely too much to say that the tone of the entire second part, considered as Gray's description of himself, is that of . . . sentimental and lachrymose self-pity." [9] Other critics have resented Gray's introduction of himself on formal grounds. R. W. Ketton-Cremer writes: "The personal element, suddenly and unhappily introduced in these lines [93 ff.], conflicts with the sober and reasoned beauty of all that has preceded them." [10] Because the circumstances of Gray's burial and the epitaph on his tomb were felt to be so tenuously related to the preceding stanzas and because the transition from the humble graves to "the poet's own imagined fate" was felt to be so abrupt, the claim has even been made that the poem really ends at line 92 with "Ev'n in our Ashes live their wonted Fires." This claim was first made by pseudo-Johnson, who concluded his criticism of the twenty-third stanza by saying, "What now remains of the Elegy, partakes of the nature of an After-piece." And his description of this "After-piece" as "rather *adhering* to the Elegy than uniting with it" recalls Walter Savage Landor's deprecation of the poem for "the tin-kettle of an epitaph tied to its tail." [11] A similar division of the poem has been made by Sir Herbert Grierson and J. C. Smith: "The stately argument moves steadily on from the lovely hushed opening to the

[9] "A Youth to Fortune and to Fame unknown," *MP*, xx (1923), 350.

[10] *Thomas Gray*, pp. 48–49. Cf. D. C. Tovey, *Gray's English Poems* (London, 1898), p. 166: "the 'personal note' with which a very general theme is made to end is distinctly not effective."

[11] *A Criticism on the Elegy* . . . , pp. 73–74; John Forster, *Walter Savage Landor, a Biography* (London, 1869), ii, 422.

wistful close: 'On some fond breast the parting soul relies.' 'The close,' we call it, for here the real elegy ends. The lines that follow about the poet's own imagined fate are fanciful by comparison." [12] Even without asking what is meant by the "real" elegy, it can be seen that here, as John Scott said of another misrepresentation of the *Elegy*, "the Critic has made the nonsense which he censures."

On the assumption that the latter part of the poem describes the life and premature death of an "unknown" peasant-poet, all the difficulties imagined to result from the intrusion of "the personal element" simply vanish. Indeed it is hardly credible that Thomas Gray, who refused to allow his name to appear in print without the protective prefix of *Mr.*, could be imagined to boast in verse that he was wise, pious, generous, and sincere. An anonymous writer in the *Quarterly Review* for 1876 seems more plausible. In the *Elegy,* he said, "as indeed in all that Gray ever wrote we find it his first principle *to prefer his subject to himself.*" [13] The italicized words supply an exact statement of the principle on which Gray undertook the revision of the original *Stanza's wrote in a country church-yard.*

The problem of the structure of the completed poem, which is raised in the "After-piece" charge, still remains, however. The same writer in the *Quarterly Review* maintained that the two "great characteristics" of Gray's poetry were "his self-suppression and his sense of form." Yet the "form" of the *Elegy* has even been doubted to exist. Pseudo-Johnson suggested that "Perhaps the author had no particular plan at all." And Vicesimus Knox said of the poem, "It is solemn, it is picturesque: but after all, it is thought, by some, to be no more than a confused heap of splendid ideas, thrown together without order, and without proportion." [14] John Scott undertook to refute Knox and to expose the "particular plan" of the *Elegy,* but he bogged down in gratuitous efforts to show that the poem would be better if certain stanzas were rearranged.[15]

Even taking the stanzas in the order in which Gray wrote them, it is still possible to demonstrate that the poem is not destitute of plan. It

[12] *A Critical History of English Poetry,* 2nd ed. (London, 1947), p. 226.

[13] "Wordsworth and Gray," *Quart. Rev.,* CXLI (Jan., 1876), 110. The italics are in the original text.

[14] *Essays, Moral and Literary* (London, 1778), p. 95. By "some" Knox evidently meant Oliver Goldsmith, but the context makes it clear that he included himself in this category. In the 5th edition (1784) of his essays (II, 186), Knox recanted and censured Goldsmith for preferring Parnell's *Night-piece on Death* to the *Elegy.* Knox's deprecatory phrase "after all" recurs frequently in criticism of Gray. Cf. George Saintsbury, *A Short History of English Literature* (New York, 1929), p. 576: "he is, after all, but a second-rate poet," and J. Crofts, *Gray: Poetry and Prose,* p. vi: "But the *Elegy,* after all, is a complacent piece."

[15] *Critical Essays on some of the Poems of several English Poets* (London, 1785), pp. 185–246.

opens with the description of a scene: darkness closing in upon a
solitary figure in a country churchyard. Four stanzas of description
are followed by fifteen stanzas of reflections occasioned by that scene.
And this alternation of description and reflection sets a pattern which
is repeated throughout the poem and which constitutes its basic
structure, as the following analysis may serve to indicate:

Description: the churchyard (1–16).
Reflections on the scene:
   a. The rural life which the dead no longer enjoy (17–28).
   b. Admonition to the "Proud" not to mock the graves (29–44).
   c. Since wasted opportunities for good (45–65).
   d. Are balanced by wasted possibilities for evil (66–76).
Description: the rude gravestones (77–84).
Reflections on the "psychology" of dying (85—92).
Description: the Stonecutter's life and death (93–111).
Reflections on the Stonecutter—the "Epitaph" (112–128).

"As to description," Gray said, "I have always thought that it made
the most graceful ornament of poetry, but never ought to make the
subject." [16] Applied to the *Elegy* this means that the descriptive parts
simply supply an "ornamental" background for the reflections which
constitute the real "subject" of the poem. It must be recognized that
the *Elegy* is not simply a loco-descriptive poem, but a philosophical
poem or, as Gray would have said, a poem of "moral reflections."

The theme of these reflections may best be approached by isolating
the basic contrast of the poem. This, of course, is primarily a class
distinction. The ruling classes are contrasted with the rural proletariat.
This contrast is developed mainly in terms of the differing burial
customs of the two classes: "The Boast of Heraldry" is contrasted with
"The short and simple Annals of the Poor," the "fretted Vault" with
"the Lap of Earth," "storied Urn" with "shapeless Sculpture," flattering elegies with "uncouth Rhimes." Attitudes toward the two classes
are developed through the Spokesman, who, as suggested before,
identifies himself with neither class. It is the Spokesman, not the
burghers nor the villagers, who is represented to be class-conscious. And
his attitude toward the two classes is fairly complicated. It is not
simply that he represents the burial customs of the rich as ostentatious,
hypocritical, and vulgar and those of the poor as simple, sincere, and
therefore pathetic, although these attitudes are present at various
points in the poem. In order to discover the Spokesman's total attitude
it is necessary to reconsider the structure of the poem.

The Spokesman's imaginative reconstruction of the lives led by the
rustics is followed by his admonishing the "Proud" not to mock be-

[16] *Correspondence of Gray,* III, 1140.

cause these lives have run their course in absolute obscurity. "Th'
inevitable Hour" awaits both rich and poor; both "The Paths of
Glory" and the "noiseless . . . Way" of the poor terminate in death,
and afterwards the only difference lies in the expensiveness of the
funeral arrangements. In this part of the poem (lines 33–44) elaboration of ceremony is represented as futile and indecorous: Death turns
a cold ear to "Flatt'ry" and no "storied Urn" has power to recall
"the fleeting Breath." Yet a certain minimum of ceremony is represented as necessary and decent. It is not the fault of the rustics that
"Mem'ry" raises no "Trophies" over their tombs; they cannot afford it.
Nevertheless they erect "Some frail Memorial" to protect their bones
from "Insult" or desecration. For no one ever died, the Spokesman
argues, without fearing that he would be forgotten and hoping to be
remembered.

> Ev'n from the Tomb the Voice of Nature cries,
> Ev'n in our Ashes live their wonted Fires.

The fiery desire for Fame is so strong that it is even imagined to
smoulder in the ashes of the dead.[17] And it smoulders in rich and
poor alike. The two classes which were so sharply contrasted are
brought together in the universality of man's desire to be known and
remembered. In retrospect, therefore, even the half-acre tombs of the
"Proud" participate in the pathos.[18]

The theme of the poem cannot be set down simply as "Death the
Leveller," for the implication is clearly that if the burial customs of the
two classes differ only in degree of elaboration, there must be other
similarities between them. As Roger Martin has said, "il s'agit moins de
l'égalité des hommes dans la mort que de l'égalité des hommes sur
terre." [19] Insignificant differences between the two classes simply
emphasize their essential similarity. Men are everywhere pretty much
alike and social rank is a mere lottery, a matter of chance:

> Th'Applause of list'ning Senates to command,
> The Threats of Pain and Ruin to despise,
> &c., &c.,
> Their *Lot* forbade: . . .

Talent and ability are distributed among the classes, not confined to
one, but the creative and governing abilities of the poor are thwarted
by lack of education. Even those peasants who are not lacking in
"Science"—native wisdom—are deprived of the historical perspective
which is gained only through education—"Knowledge . . . Rich with

---

[17] Cf. Propertius IV, 74: "haec cura et cineri spirat inusta meo."
[18] Cf. Brooks, p. 27.
[19] *Essai sur Gray* (London and Paris, 1934), p. 419.

the Spoils of Time." Moral qualities are likewise distributed *among* the classes. The poem ascribes no moral superiority to the peasants. Their progress in vice *and* virtue is simply limited by lack of scope. The village patriot withstands only the petty encroachments of a tyrannical neighbor while even the village bully cannot lay waste a whole country and the lives of its inhabitants.[20]

Obviously the Spokesman is not angry that these conditions exist. His melancholy contemplation of the unrealized virtues buried in the village churchyard is balanced by his ironic recognition of the buried vices. In fact this "balance" is one of the outstanding features of the poem. It can be seen most clearly in the Spokesman's representation of the lives of the villagers. There are no sentimentalities about the pathetic plight of the downtrodden peasant and there are no romantic delusions about "Plain living and high thinking." The extremes of bathos and unreality are rigorously avoided. The "Joys" of living on a farm are presented, but so are the sorrows. Even "the blazing Hearth" cannot take off the "chill" of poverty. If the teamsters are sometimes "jocund," the glebe is still "stubborn" and the plowman's way is "weary." There is balance even in the "consolation" which the Spokesman extends to the village dead: if they were denied Fame, they were also denied infamy; if they were denied "Glory," they were also denied "ignoble Strife." But this balance is easily upset, particularly when the poem is interpreted as a political tract. And it has been interpreted *both* as rightist and as leftist propaganda. Actually the poem is concerned neither with amelioration nor with acceptance of the condition of the rural worker. It is concerned with Fame: Fame on earth, worldly "Success," "Glory," contrasted with "fame in Heav'n." If the poem seems egalitarian, it is only to make the point that all men are equal in their desire to be known and remembered. Pseudo-Johnson's proscriptive irony is literally true: "the political creed of Thomas Gray had nothing to do in the Elegy written in a Country Churchyard."

The Spokesman's attitude toward the rustics implies that society is an organism in which all members perform useful functions and that individual ability and virtue exist where you find them. But when the *Elegy* came to be read by *doctrinaires* who believed that the aristocracy performed no function in society and that ability and virtue were to be found only among the lower and middle classes, it seemed to be a revolutionary poem. It can be no accident that the *Elegy* was translated by one after another French revolutionist from 1788 to 1805. So it is apparently ridiculous to claim, as William Empson has done, that

---

[20] The poem does not assume "an uniform innocence in humble life," as John Scott claimed. All it assumes is that village vices are "confined"—they cannot affect as many people as the vices of the powerful. . . .

the poem inculcates acquiescence in the "Lot" of the downtrodden peasant. It seems doubtful that Philippe Antoine Merlin de Douai, President of the Convention, Joseph Dusaulchoy, revolutionary publicist and editor of the suppressed journal *Le Républicain,* Pierre Cabanis, physician to Mirabeau, friend to Franklin, and public health administrator, Antoine de Cournand, the revolutionary *abbé* who publicly attacked clerical celibacy and privately took a wife, and Marie-Joseph Chénier, member of the original club of Jacobins and tragic-dramatist of the revolution, would all have translated the *Elegy* if it really demanded that "we ought to accept the injustice of society." [21]

Empson's evidence for this is his interpretation of the "Flower born to blush unseen" metaphor. Here is what he says of this stanza: [See Empson, p. 109, from "By comparing. . . ." to "unspotted from the World."] The gem-and-flower metaphor is actually introduced into the poem by the reflection that "Perhaps in this neglected Spot is laid/Some Heart once pregnant with celestial Fire, &c.," but "Chill Penury repress'd their noble Rage,/And froze the genial Current of the Soul." The metaphor which follows is alleged to afford an illustration from nature of the blighted development of the peasantry. On this view, however, the metaphor is meaningless, for both gem and flower have already achieved perfection. The gem is stated to be of the "purest" water and the flower has already bloomed. If the metaphor were to illustrate what Empson says it does, the diamond would have to remain a carbon crystal and the flower be frost-nipped in the bud. The real subject of the metaphor is Fame. All that gem and flower lack is publicity. The gem never became the Great Mogul diamond and the flower was never painted by Watteau. Presumably this is a matter of indifference to gems and flowers, but it is a matter of great importance to men. The desire for Fame is called a madness in the poem, but it is a magnificent madness, a "noble Rage," which recalls a similar ambivalence in *Lycidas:* "That last infirmity of Noble mind." The gem and flower in the metaphor are types of unrecognized potentiality, not of blighted development. But this potentiality is only unrecognized by an acquisitive society which consumes flowers and gems. And, as John Beresford has pointed out, "In 'the bosom' of God, 'Some heart once pregnant with celestial fire' and some 'flower . . . born to blush unseen' are just as important as the flowers and genius which are the subject of fame." [22] It seems doubtful, therefore, that the fact that the flower was "born" to blush unseen really implies that some men of genius must necessarily remain in ignorance and

---

[21] That the poem was equally popular with royalist sympathizers cannot be ignored. . . .

[22] "The Author of the *Elegy,*" *Edinburgh Rev.,* CCXLIV (1926), 132.

obscurity. In fact, the metaphor might be twisted around to prove that whereas minerals and vegetables can achieve perfection without "education," men cannot. So far from making the social arrangement seem "inevitable," the metaphor can just as easily make it seem intolerable. But this would be to emphasize the contrast implicit in the figure, whereas it is the comparison that is dominant. The "Gem of purest Ray serene" is an exact correlative for the "Heart once pregnant with celestial Fire." Both gem and heart have something in them of divine. And this is the real basis of the metaphor. The perfected gem and the unperfected heart go unrecognized by man; they lack Fame. But since this fire is "celestial," the presumption exists that it will be assuaged in heaven.

It is here that the full significance of the Stonecutter may be seen. The imagined death of the peasant-poet supplies the dramatic example which illustrates and makes cogent the large generalities of the previous argument. The case-history of the village Stonecutter should make the reader *feel* what previously the poem simply *stated,* namely, what it is to be a poet *manqué,* a "mute inglorious Milton" possessed of a "noble Rage" which is drowned in poverty, ignorance, lack of sympathy and scope. On the contrary, it has been claimed that the history of the Stonecutter is really two disparate works which have been clumsily thrown together to piece out some sort of conclusion for the poem. The evidence for this is said to lie in the fact that there are disparities between the two accounts that are given of the Stonecutter, one by the aged Swain and the other in the "Epitaph." But it has never been pointed out that these disparities are deliberate and dramatic. The illiterate old rustic is unsympathetic. His disapproval has been softened no doubt by death, but it is still apparent that to him the Stonecutter seemed lazy, queer, unsociable, and probably crazy. But the "Epitaph" enables the reader to see around this characterization. For the Spokesman, who composed the "Epitaph," is an outlander, a fellow *poeta ignotus,* and therefore sympathetic. He enables the reader to see that the Stonecutter was alienated from his fellow-rustics because "Fair Science frown'd not on his humble Birth/And Melancholy mark'd him for her own": intelligence and melancholic sensitivity set him apart from the "jocund" teamsters and the garrulous old Swain who thought him crazy. And if the old rustic's attitude is representative of public opinion in the village, it is not difficult to appreciate the importance of the "Friend" whom the Stonecutter "gain'd from Heav'n." Yet despite the distance between them, the Stonecutter never failed to honor the rustics' graves with a "frail Memorial." He responded to their lack of understanding with generosity and compassion, which is simply the classic situation of the Poet *vis-à-vis* Society. The workaday world may ridicule the Poet's idleness and scorn his "wayward Fancies," but human nature still cries out, even from the tomb, to be known and interpreted. And this demand is met by the Poet. So the Stonecutter "gave to Mis'ry all he had, a Tear," in the form of "uncouth Rhimes." He was not, however, without his "Frailties"—and here the poem achieves its final balance. But there is obviously no suggestion that he was "better off without opportunities." The unrealization of his "noble Rage" is presented as pathetic and his premature death as tragic.

But in the "Epitaph" he achieves a measure of remembrance. He remains "to Fortune and to Fame unknown," for true remembrance is "no plant that grows on mortal soil." He is celebrated anonymously, but the bare fact of his celebration indicates that the tradition of poetry in a world which is largely indifferent to it has been continued. So far from being an extraneous tin-kettle tied to the tail of a "stately" but rather "complacent" poem, the "Epitaph" is actually the conclusion of a very tightly-organized rhetorical structure. It supplies perspective and sympathy for the character whose life illustrates everything the poem has to say. It does not supply a judgment or a solution, for the village-Lycidas is dead and his case can only be referred to the "perfet witness of all-judging *Jove*."

3. Conclusion

The chief barrier to the understanding of the *Elegy*, aside from the preoccupations introduced by the biographical fallacy, must lie in its diction. Even Goldsmith, who wrote in the same poetic idiom, complained that the *Elegy* is "overloaded with epithet." And Wordsworth put Gray "at the head of those who . . . have attempted to widen the space of separation betwixt Prose and Metrical Composition." [23] It is not certain, however, that Gray would not have been flattered by Wordsworth's comment. For Wordsworth assumed that the language "really" used by rustics was Prose and that poetry should deviate from this standard as little as possible. The effects of this theory on Wordsworth's own poetry could be disastrous:

> The Pair had but one inmate in their house,
> An only Child, who had been born to them
> When Michael, telling o'er his years, began
> To deem that he was old,—in shepherd's phrase,
> With one foot in the grave.

Gray, on the other hand, supposed that "the language of the age is never the language of poetry" and that poetry "has a language peculiar

[23] *The Prose Works of William Wordsworth*, ed., Alexander B. Grosart (London, 1876), II, 85.

to itself; to which almost everyone, that has written, has added something by enriching it with foreign idioms and derivatives."[24] So Gray's rustic, the ancient Swain, is made to speak no "shepherd's phrase" but the language of pastoral swains from Theocritus to Pope. Although it is clearly distinguishable from the Spokesman's urbane diction by such colloquialisms as "Hard by yon Wood" (accompanied no doubt by the jerk of a horny thumb), the speech of the old rustic is a dense texture of literary allusion. As soon as this is recognized, his speech takes on an additional dimension which would be unattainable on Wordsworth's theory. As a result, the Stonecutter is not simply an imaginary rural eccentric, like the shadowy old gaffers in *The Excursion,* but also a many-dimensional figure in a series of literary characterizations reaching back to Theocritus' Thyrsis. He is characterized not simply by the words spoken by the Swain but also by the allusions to Corydon, Colin Cloute, etc., which these words suggest. He becomes, in short, the representative Poet.

It is not surprising, therefore, that Wordsworth should have found the language of the *Elegy* unintelligible. The two poets disagree on nearly every point of literary theory. Wordsworth, for example, declared that by looking steadily at his "subject" he had gained "one property of all good poetry, namely, good sense," but that this practice necessarily cut him off from "the phrases and figures of speech which have long been regarded as the common inheritance of Poets."[25] Gray, on the contrary, insisted that "Sense is nothing in poetry, but according to the dress she wears, & the scene she appears in."[26] He recognized that "cold good sense" can make a sorry figure when stripped of its "common inheritance." I. A. Richards attributes the "triumph" of the *Elegy* to Gray's perfect adjustment of "his familiar feelings toward the subject and his awareness of the inevitable triteness of the only possible reflections, to the discriminating attention of his audience."[27] Gray was *enabled* to express moral commonplaces in the *Elegy* without "faults of tone" precisely because the conventional diction of the poem proclaims in every line that these commonplaces are recognized as such. When Wordsworth expresses similar ideas in the "language really used by men" the uneasy feeling is aroused either that Wordsworth does not know how trite his commonplaces are or, worse, that he thinks he invented them himself. The "random truths" of poetry, as Wordsworth calls them, are almost certain to be commonplaces. "Their character as commonplaces," to quote Richards again, "does not make them any less important, and the Elegy may usefully

[24] *Correspondence of Gray,* I, 192.
[25] *Prose Works of Wordsworth,* II, 84.
[26] *Correspondence of Gray,* II, 593.
[27] *Practical Criticism* (New York, 1929), p. 207.

remind us that boldness and originality are not necessities of great poetry. But these thoughts and feelings, in part because of their significance and nearness to us are peculiarly difficult to express without faults of tone," that is, either high-pitched overstatement or elliptical evasion. Poetry is not made simply by uttering random truths. And it seems almost certain that the great commonplaces are nothing in poetry but according to the dress they wear and the scene they appear in.

Wordsworth claimed that the mere appearance in a poem of "POETIC DICTION" guarantees that the "emotion" is either false or nonexistent. In Wordsworth's view the *Elegy* is simply a "mechanical" exercise in the application of ornamental diction to a conventional theme. The biographical fallacy, at the opposite extreme, represents the poem as "a passionate piece of autobiography." [28] But neither interpretation is adequate. The former dismisses Gray because he was "curiously elaborate in the structure of his . . . poetic diction" without asking what are the rhetorical effects of this elaboration. And the latter culminates in nonsense about Gray's excessive piety and lachrymosity. If the poem is "autobiography," it would have to be concluded that "He gave to Mis'ry all he had, a Tear," whereas it is a matter of legal record that Gray left ten pounds to be distributed to "honest and industrious poor Persons" in the parish of Stoke Poges.

The classical statement of the theory underlying the biographical fallacy occurs in Sainte-Beuve's *Nouveaux lundis*:

> La littérature, la production littéraire n'est point pour moi distincte ou du moins séparable du reste de l'homme et de l'organisation; je puis goûter une œuvre, mais il m'est difficile de la juger indépendamment de la connaissance de l'homme même; et je dirais volontiers: *tel arbre, tel fruit*. L'étude littéraire me mène ainsi tout naturellement à l'étude morale.[29]

> [For me literature, literary works are not at all distinct or, at any rate, separable from the rest of the man and his individuality; I can appreciate a work, but it is difficult for me to judge it independently from my knowledge of the man himself; and I willingly say: "by their fruits ye shall know them." Thus literary study leads me quite naturally to psychological study.]

Aside from the disadvantage which would accrue to criticism if it were debarred from judging the *Iliad*, the *Chanson de Roland*, and *King Lear* (to mention but three works about whose authors and their moral *organisation* nothing is known), there is an obvious fallacy in

---

[28] A. C. Benson, "The Secret of Gray," *Poetry Rev.*, VII (1916), 388.
[29] (Paris, 1865), III, 15. . . .

the analogy *tel arbre, tel fruit.* It is simply the *argumentum ad hominem* in a horticultural guise. The Muses award no prize for good behavior. And to the despair of the moralists, the fact remains that great literature has been written by depraved and reprobate characters. The evidence of existing criticism of Gray's *Elegy* seems to emphasize the opposite of Sainte-Beuve's argument: that it is *essential* to judge a literary work "indépendamment de la connaissance de l'homme même."

Sainte-Beuve supposed that literary studies were in the primitive stage of anatomical studies before Cuvier. So he wanted to raise them to the level of natural sciences, to establish a positive "science des esprits" through systematic and comparative study of biographical data. But it is doubtful that Saint-Beuve's expectations have been, or ever can be, realized. Increase in the knowledge of a poet's biography does not necessarily result in corresponding increases in the understanding or enjoyment of his poetry. In fact it might be argued that detailed knowledge about Wordsworth's early amatory misfeasance or his later false teeth, or Shelley's interminable plumbing difficulties, imposes a considerable barrier to delight in the poetry.

No valid argument can be made, however, against knowing all there is to know about a poet's life. And there will always be more readers to be titillated by scholarly gossip than to be harried by scholarly criticism. Nor can it be denied that biographical evidence may explain a chance allusion, clarify an occasional obscurity, or interpret a phrase. But it cannot interpret a poem. Whether it can be accepted or not, the interpretation of the *Elegy* proposed in the second part of this essay owes nothing to biographical evidence. To the extent that biographical evidence is necessary to the interpretation of a poem, the poet has failed to objectify or generalize his private experience. So the effectiveness of a poem may be said to vary inversely with the amount of biographical evidence which must be supplied for its interpretation. If the private experience is successfully generalized, however, it becomes impossible to reconstruct it from the poem, as the case of the *Elegy* shows. Where it is possible to reconstruct, from external documents, the experience that informed a poem, it is found that autobiography has been so drastically abstracted and reordered that it becomes unrecognizable as autobiography. Why, then, should it be assumed that a poet's procedure is otherwise when the experience lies beyond the possibility of reconstruction?

There are good arguments, however, to be made against mixing what is known about a poet's life into the interpretation of his works. Gray's *Elegy* affords the "prerogative instance." Anxiety to connect the poem with the known fact of Gray's grief for his friend, Richard West, has obscured not merely the date of the poem's composition, but its "real" meaning. Montaigne's observation "Le dire est aultre chose que le faire: il fault considerer le presche à part, et le prescheur à part," [Saying is entirely different from doing; one must consider the preaching separately and the preacher separately.] is even more imperative in the present context.

There are equally good arguments against the acceptance of poetic utterance as biographical fact. A poem cannot even be accepted as reliable evidence of a state of mind, much less of a position of body. This is shown by such typical biographical aberrations as "the mythical sorrows of Shakespeare" [30] invented by Freidrich Schlegel and endlessly elaborated, or Wordsworth's "moral crisis" of 1795 which was devised by Emile Legouis solely from "internal evidence" in *The Prelude*. Instead of *tel arbre, tel fruit,* what is needed is a view of poetry which sees in Gray's *Elegy* neither an autobiographical document nor a literary exercise, but a calculated rhetorical structure—calculated, that is, to produce certain intellectual and emotional effects on a reader. The job of criticism then becomes to make it as clear as possible what these effects are, not *sub specie aeternitatis,* but on the critic himself. In this view, criticism can resume its original Aristotelian function of rhetorical analysis, instead of pretending to dictate terms to poetry or to serve as a substitute for it.

Coleridge complained that he was led "by Mr. Wordsworth's conversation" to discover faults in the *Elegy* which he had formerly considered "as proof against all fair attacks." But the context makes it clear that these were "faults" of diction again. And Coleridge found that when he had reexamined the poem with impartial strictness to see "whether the collective meaning was sense or nonsense," his effort was more than repaid by the "additional delight" which he experienced.[31] The legitimate function of criticism is to make it possible to read the *Elegy* with "additional delight." For Gray himself said that "even a bad verse [is] as good a thing or better, than the best observation, that was ever made upon it."

[30] C. J. Sisson, "The Mythical Sorrows of Shakespeare," *Annual Shakespeare Lecture of the British Academy* (London, 1934).

[31] *Biographia Literaria,* ed., J. Shawcross (Oxford, 1907), 1, 26, n.

Gray's "Epitaph" Revisited

by Morse Peckham

Several years ago Dr. Frank E. Ellis published an illuminating essay on Gray's *Elegy Written in a Country Church-Yard* [pp. 51ff.]. Yet he left certain problems unsolved. In the present paper I shall confine myself solely to the dramatic structure, the topography, and to the action, real and imagined, in order to answer the question, "Who wrote 'The Epitaph'?"

On the opening lines, Ellis quotes John Hill, one of the first critics: "Let us recollect the situation of the poet, in a still evening, contemplating, from an elevated spot, the country round him, while there is scarce light for the prospect" (p. 989). Hill is surely correct. The Spokesman is high enough above the lea to see the herd *winding* across it, to observe the landscape, and, perhaps, to see the distant folds. Somewhere nearby is the tower: the simplest explanation of lines 9 to 12 is that it is the Spokesman himself who is molesting the owl's reign. Certainly, he is not *at* the tower, nor *in* the graveyard: "those" elms and "that" yew-tree indicate that he is not in the latter, a fact emphasized by the parallel construction of these phrases with "yonder" tower.

Line 45, however, indicates either that Gray is inconsistent or that the position of the Spokesman has changed. "This neglected Spot" plainly indicates that he is now *in* the churchyard. To be sure, it may be argued that the graveyard, since he may imagine as well as actually see the graves, has become so real to him that he can refer to it by "this." However, the principle of economy should hold in this as in all kinds of analysis: unnecessary complications should not be introduced. The simpler interpretation is that the Spokesman, during his "reflections on the Scene" (Ellis, 998), has moved from the hillside or elevated spot to the churchyard itself. Lines 77 to 84 confirm this interpretation. If "still" is translated as "always" rather than "yet," the passage can be phrased thus: "Despite the unimportance of such people, someone always erects memorials to protect

"Gray's 'Epitaph' Revisited," by Morse Peckham. From Modern Language Notes, *LXXI (1956), 409–11. Copyright © 1956* Modern Language Notes *(Johns Hopkins University). Reprinted by permission of the editor.*

their graves from insult and to appeal to the sympathy of the passer-by."

In line 93 enters the Stonecutter-Poet, Ellis' most important and most disputed contribution to the interpretation of the poem. Surely, that this figure is in the poem can scarcely be denied. The question is how and when he is there. As for the first problem, he exists only in the imagination of the Spokesman, nor must this fact be forgotten for a moment. And as a projection of the Spokesman's imagination, he is very much like him, alienated from Society. In the same way, the Kindred Spirit is a projection with a similar personality. There remains the question of time. "Dost" indicates that the Spokesman imagines the Stonecutter to be living at the time of the former's monologue, while "shall inquire" suggests that the Spokesman imagines the imaginary Stonecutter's death as a future event, to occur after the Spokesman's visit and after the poem's utterance.

In the same way as he has invented the Stonecutter and the Kindred Spirit, the Spokesman now imagines the hoary-headed Swain, an illiterate old man who describes the Stonecutter in language filled with literary echoes. No language could be more appropriate, for the Swain is a projection of the Spokesman, himself a literary and cultivated individual. It is proper for him to imagine the Swain's speech in terms of the pastoral tradition; for the Spokesman has a very lively imagination. He imagines the imaginary Swain guiding an imaginary enquirer, the Kindred Spirit, to an imaginary epitaph. And this leads to the right question. It is not, "Who wrote the 'Epitaph'?" It cannot be the Spokesman, who imagines the "Epitaph," and in this sense only composes it as part of his meditation. The right question is, "Who is it that the Spokesman imagines will write the 'Epitaph'?" The answer lies in line 124: "He gain'd from Heav'n ('twas all he wish'd) a Friend." And the fact that the Spokesman imagines it accounts for the literary flavor; it is not in the least crude, as it would have been had the Spokesman been reading a real epitaph inspired by "th' unletter'd Muse."

There remains a further question important to this problem. What is the relation of the poem to the title? After Gray's time this kind of poem came to be called a dramatic monologue. The title provides the frame, or setting. It is not Gray who wrote an elegy in Stoke Poges, but an imaginary poet invented by Gray who composes a poem in an unidentified graveyard. Gray imagines the anonymous Poet, who is the Spokesman.

To sum up, the Poet-Spokesman moves from a hillside to the churchyard, examines the tombstones, imagines the local Stonecutter-Poet whose function it is to compose epitaphs and carve them, imagines an inquirer who will ask about him after his death sometime in the future, imagines the Swain who will be asked, imagines the epitaph that will be written for the Stonecutter, and imagines the Friend who will write it and who, perhaps, will succeed him as village epitaph-writer and carver.

Analyzed in this way, the dramatic structure and the imaginative levels of the poem are perfectly clear and exquisitely realized.

The Stonecutter in Gray's "Elegy"

by John H. Sutherland

In a recent note Professor Morse Peckham supports the now popular thesis that the epitaph in Gray's "Elegy" refers to the "stonecutter-poet" who is obliquely adumbrated in the twentieth and twenty-first stanzas.[1] This interpretation seems to have been first suggested by Professor Herbert Starr in 1949 and to have been independently supported by Dr. Frank Ellis two years later. It is the purpose of the present paper to attempt to disprove this interpretation. [The author summarizes Shepard's identification of the "Youth to Fortune and to Fame Unknown" with Richard West and points out that the problem centers on the ambiguous references in ll. 93–94.]

In 1949 Professor Herbert Starr's "Re-estimation" of Professor Shepard's article attacked Shepard's conclusions by pointing out that his argument is based on little more than speculation; that there is no solid textual or biographical evidence to demonstrate that Gray was writing about West. His own suggested reading combines Shepard's *Ignotus* and *poeta*. He suggests that "Gray is representing an unappreciated young *village* poet," but he does not insist that the village poet be a real, historical person. He also suggests that the phrase "these lines" may refer to the "uncouth rhimes" on the gravestones.[2]

Although Professor Peckham credits Ellis with first suggesting that Gray intended to refer to a "stonecutter-poet," it seems clear that this proposal of Starr's is an earlier version of the same theory. Professor Peckham accepts this identification of "thee" and "these lines" but refines on it by suggesting that the poem as a whole is a dramatic monologue, in which an imaginary "Poet-Spokesman . . . imagines the local Stonecutter-Poet."[3] This seems an improvement over some earlier, more personal and romantic, readings of the poem, since it is in accord with the common eighteenth-century device of using a

---

"The Stonecutter in Gray's 'Elegy,'" by John H. Sutherland. From Modern Philology, *LV (1957), 11–13.* Copyright © 1957 by Modern Philology. *Reprinted by permission of the editor.*

[1] Peckham, pp. 76–78.
[2] Starr, p. 44.
[3] Peckham, p. 77.

fictional narrator in order to achieve objectivity. However, it leaves us with the controversial stonecutter-poet as the antecedent of "thee" in line 93 and as the subject of the epitaph.

In the Eton MS, the equivalents of lines 93–94 are: "And thou, who mindful of th' unhonour'd Dead/Dost in these Notes their artless Tale relate. . . ."[4] In this early version of the poem, which Gray never published, there is no doubt that "thou" and "these Notes" refer, respectively, to the narrator and to the "Elegy" itself. There is no possibility of confusion or ambiguity because the stonecutter does not enter the poem in any way.

As Dr. Ellis has shown, Gray made the poem more impersonal in revision by changing pronoun references in several places; but there is no real evidence that Gray wished to change the reference of either "thee" or "these lines." It does violence to grammar and logic to read "thee" as referring to a stonecutter who is not even mentioned in the poem—whose existence is only indirectly suggested by the abstract phrase, "th' unletter'd muse." Similarly, one must stretch common sense to the limit to make "these lines" refer to "uncouth rhimes" mentioned four stanzas before—rhymes which are described as being so short and rough that they provide nothing more than "names" and "years" instead of "fame and elegy."

Moreover, the epitaph does not fit this shadowy stonecutter at all well. For example, what would partisans of the stonecutter do with line 119: *"Fair Science frown'd not on his humble birth"*? This would seem to refer to someone a little better educated than an artisan inspired by "th' unletter'd muse." Ellis, it is true, attempts to meet this objection by arguing that the word "science" in this instance refers to native intelligence.[5] However, the *OED* does not record examples of such usage. If Gray did intend "science" to mean no more than intelligence or ability, it is the only occasion in which he used the word in such a sense. Professor Albert S. Cook's *Concordance to the English Poems of Thomas Gray* lists four other poems in which Gray uses the word "science"; in each of these the word seems quite clearly to refer to knowledge gained as the result of education.[6] There is no reason to think that Gray would use the word in an almost opposite sense in the "Elegy." It is difficult to imagine that he could have meant the epitaph to refer to a person inspired by "th' unletter'd muse," since he would surely have felt that "Fair Science" had frowned on such a person's birth.

Some readers have been eager to find a subject other than the narrator for the epitaph because the tone of the poem seems unpleasant

[4] *The Works of Thomas Gray,* ed., Edmund Gosse (London, 1884), I, 77.
[5] Ellis, p. 70.
[6] Boston and New York, 1908, p. 114.

if it is read as applying to Gray himself. However, as Professor Peckham and others have pointed out, the epitaph can properly be read as referring to a fictional narrator, and—if we think of the "Elegy" as the meditation of this narrator—"these lines" can be read as referring to the poem as a whole. There is one possible difficulty with this interpretation: it is in the apparent shift in point of view from the "me" of the first stanza to the "thcc" of line 93. Professor Cleanth Brooks seems to accept the case for a fictional narrator and explains the shift as dramatic in nature.[7] If read in this way, the shift reveals that the speaker is viewing himself objectively, that he has started to think of himself with the same sorts of feeling that he has previously expressed about the inhabitants of the graveyard. Thus the shift may be construed as an appropriate introduction to the speech of the "hoary-headed swain" and to the epitaph itself.

The character of the narrator can be drawn, in general terms, from the poem: he posed as "Il Penseroso" (ll. 98–108); he dreamed of dying young and never making a name for himself (ll. 93ff.); he was well educated (l. 119), charitable (l. 121), and sentimental (*passim*). Certainly Professor Shepard was right in feeling that this narrator may have had personal origins involving West as well as Gray himself. However, these origins merely furnished raw material from which an impersonal figure was evolved. In the final poetic structure Gray almost certainly did not wish the narrator to resemble any specific person. All that can be said is that the narrator and the subject of the epitaph are the same person and that that person is described as an educated young gentleman, not as an unlettered village stonecutter.

[7] Brooks, p. 28.

The Ambivalence of Gray's Elegy

by A. E. Dyson

The prevailing impression we have on considering Gray's *Elegy* in retrospect is of its distinctive "atmosphere," contemplative and Horatian. There is the stoic reflection on the transcience of earthly glory that we associate with this tradition, the same apparent preference for a Sabine Farm, "far from the madding crowd's ignoble strife." The gentle melancholy of the mood, as well as the syntax of stanzas 24 and 25, points to Gray himself as the subject of the "Epitaph." It expresses a wish which, in this particular mood, he has for his whole future: to be "marked out" by melancholy for her own, to live and die in peaceful rustic security.

But this is by no means all that the *Elegy* says, and it ignores some powerful emotional undercurrents. For Gray is seeing the "rude Forefathers" of the hamlet in two rôles simultaneously, both as the happiest of men, and as victims. The plowman in stanza 1 is "weary," the slumbering dead are rude and unlettered. The tombs "with uncouth rhimes and shapeless sculptures deck'd" implore the passing tribute of a sigh as much for their uncouthness as for the death of their inmates. The obscurity of country life has restrained and killed the innate potentialities of the rustics, for good as well as for evil. Not only is the possible Cromwell comparatively guiltless, but the possible Milton is mute and inglorious, both forbidden by their lot any spectacular fulfilment. The obscurity, therefore, in which their happiness is supposed to consist is felt in terms of waste. The words "mute" and "inglorious" acquire an ambiguity from their context. They are words of deprivation and defeat, but they are here levelled up by juxtaposition with the "guiltless" Cromwells almost to the status of happiness.

This basic ambivalence reveals conflicting emotional responses to the situation of the rustics, and these responses develop side by side

---

"*The Ambivalence of Gray's Elegy*," by A. E. Dyson. *From* Essays in Criticism, ed., F. W. Bateson (Oxford), VII (1957), 257–61. Copyright © 1957 by F. W. Bateson. *Reprinted by permission of F. W. Bateson.*

as the poem progresses. From the Horatian viewpoint, the rude forefathers are more to be envied than pitied. Pomfret in his *Choice*
asked little more from life (except, perhaps, the "philosophic mind"),
and Lady Chudworth in her *Resolve* wanted only

> A soul, which cannot be depressed by grief,
> Nor too much rais'd by the sublimest joy.

The Augustan quest for the golden mean excluded extremes of
either emotion or achievement, and looked for happiness in detach-
ment from the busy world of men. Pomfret and Lady Chudworth express an attitude to life which is typical of their age, and which
survived sufficiently far into the eighteenth century to influence
Gray. From this point of view, the lot of the "forefathers" in the *Elegy*
is little short of ideal.

> Far from the madding crowd's ignoble strife,
> Their sober wishes never learn'd to stray:
> Along the cool sequester'd vale of life
> They kept the noiseless tenor of their way.

In this and other stanzas Gray expresses a rational approval of the
rustic life, and in the "Epitaph" he identifies himself, in wish-fulfil-
ment, with it. The youth "to fortune and to fame unknown" is not
unlike Tennyson's Lady of Shalott before her choice—a legend to all
men, but known to none. He represents, like Arnold's Scholar Gipsy
after him, the ideal of a serene and untroubled existence—but an
existence which is essentially an escape from life as we know it into
a state less vulnerable to the "thousand natural shocks that flesh is
heir to." The peace which he enjoys is nearer to death than to life,
more like defeat than victory.

The contradiction inherent in this becomes clear as we notice that
the rude forefathers, even while they are being offered to us as an
ideal, are also being represented as victims, both of society and of the
nature of things. The primary meanings of "mute" and "inglorious"
suggest this, and there is a sense in which the extremism of the
Miltons and Cromwells, whether good or bad ethically, is seen as good
in so far as it is fulfilment, expression, achievement, "life abundant."
The "applause of listening Senates," the despising of dangers, the
"scattering of plenty o'er a smiling land" are positive and vital touch-
stones, beside which the rustic life is felt as a tragic waste. The rude
forefathers were victims of a political system which forbade them
their proper fulfilment. The "genial current of their soul" was frozen
by "Chill Penury." The hearts once "pregnant with celestial fire" are
now laid, unhonoured and unremembered, "in some neglected spot."
The creative spirit was there, but it found no opportunity for expres-

sion. There is, in this reflection, a profound awareness of waste. Death is so cold and irrevocable (stanza 11), beauty so fleeting and futile (stanza 14). The rustic moralist may have been taught by his simple religion how to die, but ought he not rather to have been given a chance to live?

> For who to dumb forgetfulness a prey,
> This pleasing anxious being e'er resigned,
> Left the warm precincts of the cheerful day,
> Nor cast one longing, lingering look behind?

It is to be noted that the enemy to man's fulfilment is not only society, but Nature herself. The adjectives and verbs of the opening stanzas are narcotic and hostile: "tolls," "parting," "lowing," "plods," "weary," "fades," "glimmering," "droning," "drowsy," "lull," "moping," "complain," "secret," "molest," "ancient," "solitary," "heaves," "mouldering," "narrow cell," "rude." In stanza 7, the harvesters are at war with Nature. In stanza 14, beauty is the victim of a vast and mysterious universe; the gem lost in ocean's "dark unfathomed caves," the flower wasted upon the "desert air" which will destroy it. Finally, as the "hoary-headed swain" indicates the grave of Gray (if it *is* Gray—the syntax is not clear, but the thought indicates that it is), the nearby wood smiles "as in scorn." (The phrase "as in scorn" applies, in the first version of the poem, to the dead man, but in the final version it applies equally, by ambiguity, to the wood.) Nature, therefore, is a more primitive and dubious goddess here than in orthodox Augustan circles, and we might even discern that sense of the ruthless profusion and wastefulness of her works which has become a preoccupation with some post-Darwinian thinkers.

How far Gray was conscious of ambivalence in his *Elegy* we can probably not hope to decide. The "graveyard mood" would have seemed to him, perhaps, as unified as the style in which he expresses it. He is unlikely to have shared our present-day awareness of complexity or a tension of opposites in such a mood. Even so, the two attitudes we have been considering exist quite explicitly, side by side, in the poem, and we can legitimately speculate on the subconscious responses to life which they reveal. These would seem to have included a shrinking from life, with its menaces and responsibilities (something very like the Freudian death-wish, in fact), and also a desire for life (the almost inevitable complementary pull). In a very personal way, the "slumbering dead" must have seemed a reproach to Gray. He is aware, in the poem, of his social superiority to them. They were unlettered, he is a scholar; they had no opportunity of notable achievement, he, in his own academic sphere at least, has had it. But he has failed to take his own considerable opportunities; his vast learning was

notoriously unproductive. He is very far from having the spirit of a
Milton or a Cromwell. His letters often show him in a Hamlet-like
strain of frustration and melancholia. He is like the Hamlet of Act V,
assured of the impossibility of what he most desired, stoically resigned
to life on these terms ("There's providence in the fall of a sparrow"),
yet haunted by the futility of it all ("Alas, poor Yorrick"), and still
balancing in his mind the great alternative propositions "To be or
not to be"). All of these attitudes are present in the *Elegy,* though
with less imaginative intensity, of course, than in *Hamlet*: and so the
stanzas which approve the lot of the forefathers spring not only from
a reasoned Augustan belief in the rural life ("Let not ambition mock
their useful toil . . ."), but also from a vicarious realization of the
death-wish. And Gray's frustration is apparent not only when he is
pitying the rustics, but also when he is envying them; for it is their
death, not their life, that he envies.

Gray often seems to be seeing his relationship to the "great" as
analogous to the rustics' relationship to himself. In the final stanzas
he identifies himself with the rustics and dies to ambition and self-
fulfilment with them, but here the ambivalence of emotional response
is especially to be felt. "A youth to fortune and to fame unknown"
invites our pity; his simple contentment,

> He gained from Heaven ('twas all he wished) a friend

calls for acquiescence.

So the emotional charge of the *Elegy* is far from simple, and that
which is ostensibly offered as a good is *felt* in terms of waste. The
reflections on the rustics' death in stanzas 4–7 become, by implication,
a reflection on their life. The "lowly bed" from which they will not
again be roused is the bed on which their life has been passed. The
long silence and obscurity of the tomb is the same in kind as the
condition in which life has drifted away. Their obscurity in death
and their obscurity in life are equally symbolized by the buried gem
and the wasted flower. And death, in its dual aspect as a longed-for rest
and a dreaded waste, is present in a single image.

> Beneath those rugged elms, that yew-tree's shade,
>   Where heaves the turf in many a mould'ring heap,
> Each in his narrow cell for ever laid,
>   The rude forefathers of the hamlet sleep . . .
>
> The breezy call of incense-breathing morn,
>   The swallow twitt'ring from the straw-built shed,
> The cock's shrill clarion, or the echoing horn,
>   No more shall rouse them from their lowly bed.

Gray chooses sleep before action, like the lotus-eaters, and like Keats he is half in love with easeful death. But he also feels, with Milton's Belial, that any form of consciousness is to be preferred to oblivion, and, like Keats again, responds in some degree to a pull back to life—the "incense-breathing morn" and the clarion cock-crow.

This complexity is by no means as rich as that in the *Ode to a Nightingale,* and the desire for life receives no expression comparable in power to Keats's nightingale-symbol of ideal and eternal beauty. But it is a complexity similar in kind, if not in poetic intensity, to that realised by Keats in the *Ode,* and this may well be one of the reasons why the *Elegy* has always found a "mirror in every mind."

Gray's *Elegy* Reconsidered

by Ian Jack

The Province of Eloquence is to reign over minds of slow perception & little imagination, to set things in lights they never saw them in—to engage their attention by details & circumstances gradually unfolded, to adorn & heighten them with images & colours unknown to them to raise & engage their rude passions &c.

Gray's *Common Place Book*, iii, p. [1,111],
transcribed from the Pocket Book of 1755.

If it were not for William Mason, critics of Gray's most famous poem would have less scope for disagreement. Mason tells us that Gray

originally gave it only the simple title of "Stanzas written in a Country Church-yard." I persuaded him first to call it an ELEGY, because the subject authorized him so to do; and the alternate measure, in which it was written, seemed peculiarly fit for that species of composition.[1]

Mason complicates matters further when he tells us that he is inclined to believe that the poem was "begun, if not concluded," [2] soon after the death of Richard West. Taking their cue from Mason, subsequent critics have often associated the poem with West's death, while some have even regarded it as in a sense an elegy on Gray's early friend. As a result of this anyone who wishes to come to terms with the *Elegy* today is obliged first of all to make his own assessment of the evidence about the date of composition and the original intention of the poem.

There are two different sorts of poem: poems whose writers know from the beginning what they intend to say: and poems whose writers do not. This distinction in terms of the way in which a poem comes into existence is antecedent to distinctions of genre or "kind" in the

---

"Gray's Elegy *Reconsidered," by Ian Jack. Condensed for this edition by Mr. Jack from the complete essay in* From Sensibility to Romanticism: Essays Presented to Frederick A. Pottle *(New York: Oxford University Press, 1965), eds., Frederick W. Hilles and Harold Bloom, pp. 139–69. Copyright © 1965 by Oxford University Press. Reprinted by permission of the publisher.*

[1] *The Poems of Mr. Gray. To which are prefixed Memoirs of his Life and Writings*, 1775, p. 106.

[2] *Memoirs* (separately paged), p. 157.

more usual sense. In the first case a poet sits down to write a poem, and the result may be *To his Coy Mistress, Paradise Lost,* or *The Rape of the Lock.* In the second case a poem—or more probably a fragment of poetry—pushes a poet into a chair and makes him write, and the result may be *Kubla Khan, Endymion,* or *In Memoriam.* The traditional European Art of Poetry is based on the study of poems of the first sort—poems which may be regarded as artifacts produced by men with particular intentions in mind, so that their technique can be considered in terms of the skill with which they have attempted to achieve their ends. Romantic aesthetic is more helpful when we approach poems of the second sort, because it lays more emphasis on the spontaneous power of the poet's imagination than on questions of intention and rhetoric.

If this distinction is valid, then there are two misconceptions we must guard against. One is the assumption that the first sort of poem is typically "classical" or Augustan and the second typically "romantic" or modern. Although poems of the second sort have probably become more common in the last two centuries, it seems likely that poems of both sorts are written in most periods. The other misconception is to suppose that any given poem must be of one sort or the other, and cannot contain elements of both: that a planned poem can owe nothing to "inspiration," that an "inspired" poem can owe nothing to planning. In every great poem (on the contrary) there is almost certain to be an element of planning as well as an element of "inspiration." It is because there is no planning in *Kubla Khan* (or no planning of which the poet himself was conscious) that Coleridge was unwilling to publish it: it is because there is so little but careful planning in *Cato* that the tragedy lies unregarded in the pages of Addison's *Collected Works.*

Because we have always known Gray's poem as an Elegy—as *the* Elegy—and because it is so obviously the work of a learned poet who is superbly in control of his technique, we naturally assume that it is a poem of the planned sort; yet the little that we know or can guess about the process of its composition suggests a different view— as does a careful analysis of the poem itself.

The most important evidence about the date of composition is that contained in a letter from Gray to Horace Walpole which was written on the 12th of June 1750. Enclosing a copy of the completed poem, he wrote:

> Having put an end to a thing, whose beginning you have seen long ago, I immediately send it you. (*Correspondence,* I, 326–27.)

Since there is no question of the poem's having been begun before 1741, and since Gray and Walpole were estranged from that year until the end of 1745, "long ago" cannot refer to a date earlier than 1745–46. This would confirm Walpole's remark to Mason, when the latter was engaged on the Memoirs:

> The *Churchyard* was, I am persuaded, posterior to West's death [1742] at least three or four years. . . . At least I am sure that I had the twelve or more first lines from himself above three years after that period, and it was long before he finished it. (Yale Edition, Vol. 28, 117–18.)

The only reason for doubting this chronology is a statement in Mason's *Memoirs* which Walpole is usually considered to have accepted as a correction to his own view. After mentioning the poems that Gray wrote in August 1742, Mason continues:

> I am inclined to believe that the Elegy in a Country Church-yard was begun, if not concluded, at this time also. (*Memoirs*, p. 157.)

Here Mason appears to be speculating, on the basis of circumstantial evidence, and it may well be that he wished to prove that Gray had anticipated Shenstone's use of what came to be known as the "elegiac stanza" in 1743.[3] It is misleading of Mason to use the words "if not concluded." He immediately acknowledges that, "as it stands at present, the conclusion is of a later date," printing the earlier conclusion in his notes with the admission that Gray's "after-thought was unquestionably the best."[4] His meaning (therefore) is presumably that the earlier version was probably concluded in 1742. But if that is true, then apparently Gray waited three or four years before showing any part of the (completed) poem to anyone—then showed Walpole only about twelve lines—and then waited another four or five years before writing a new conclusion and so completing a poem now eight years old. It seems most unlikely. Gray once told West that he grew "less enamour'd" of his own productions "the older they grow,"[5] and we may well conclude that if after four years he had been dissatisfied with all but a dozen lines of a poem he would have abandoned it or at least refrained from showing so brief a fragment to Horace Walpole. Unless (therefore) important new evidence makes its appearance, I doubt whether Walpole's enigmatic remark in a letter that Mason's "account of the Elegy puts an end to my other criticism"[6] can be taken as proof that Walpole sincerely and rightly accepted all that Mason had said about the date of composition. It seems to me more likely that Walpole was referring to some different "criticism,"

[3] J. Fisher investigated the question of Gray's possible indebtedness to Shenstone in *Modern Philology*, 32 (1934–35). The suggestion of a motive on Mason's part is my own.

[4] *Poems*, p. 106.

[5] *Correspondence*, I, 196.

[6] Yale Edition, Vol. 28, p. 123.

or that he wrongly allowed himself to be persuaded by Mason, or that he was simply bored by that rather tedious man.

So we are driven back to the most likely hypothesis, that Gray began the poem about the year 1746; and there are two sentences in his letters which fit in very well. On the 10th of August 1746 he wrote to Thomas Wharton (later the recipient of one of the three MSS. of the poem which still survive):

> The Muse, I doubt, is gone, & has left me in far worse Company: if she returns, you will hear of her.

On the 11th of September he told him that he was writing "a few autumnal Verses . . . dureing the Fall of the Leaf": an apt enough description (surely) of the opening of the *Elegy*. As Thomson had written in a poem that Gray knew very well, Autumn is the time

> For those whom wisdom and whom nature charm . . .
> [To] woo lone Quiet in her silent walks. (*Autumn*, 964, 969.)

Autumn was the season when "Philosophic Melancholy" might appropriately demand ". . . the sigh for suffering worth/Lost in obscurity." (1022–23) Whether or not the first lines of the poem to be written were the initial stanzas describing sunset in the churchyard, it seems likely that the poem was born of a mood. The first few lines may even have come with a misleading spontaneity. If so, it is conceivable that Gray did not know what the poem was to be about. The opening lines merely set the scene: the only thing we can say with certainty of the poem that is to follow them is that it must be pensive and melancholy. It must be something in the vein of "Il Penseroso"—a title that Gray had already appropriated to himself in a letter to West. It is not surprising to find that he would have liked to use Virgil's famous line—

> Sunt lacrimae rerum, et mentem mortalia tangunt[7]

—as the motto of the poem, if Young had not already used it for his *Night Thoughts*.

We do not know how long it took Gray to write the earlier version of the poem, as it has come down to us.[8] The evidence of its later history, as contained in the Eton College MS., suggests that he may almost from the first have worked slowly, with many corrections. In any event, the earlier version of the poem as we have it consists of

---

[7] [The sorrows of life demand our tears, and mortal chances affect the mind.]

[8] It is most readily accessible in Appendix I of *The Poems of Gray and Collins,* ed., Austin Lane Poole, 4th ed., 1941. For the Eton College MS. see Publication Number 31 of the Augustan Reprint Society, Los Angeles, 1951, ed., George Sherburn, which also gives a facsimile of the first edition.

the first 18 stanzas of the *Elegy* as it is usually printed (in a slightly different text), followed by four further stanzas, of which three were later omitted and the fourth rewritten to become lines 93–96.

In this form the poem begins with the familiar series of stanzas in which the poet reflects that some of the humble villagers buried in the churchyard might have become famous, if they had been given the opportunity. Instead of despising them, we should reflect that it may have been their very obscurity that preserved their innocence. This leads naturally to the conclusion:

> The thoughtless World to Majesty may bow
> Exalt the brave, & idolize Success
> But more to Innocence their Safety owe
> Than Power & Genius e'er conspired to bless
>
> And thou, who mindful of the unhonour'd Dead
> Dost in these Notes their artless Tale relate
> By Night & lonely Contemplation led
> To linger in the gloomy Walks of Fate
>
> Hark how the sacred Calm, that broods around
> Bids ev'ry fierce tumultuous Passion cease
> In still small Accents whisp'ring from the Ground
> A grateful Earnest of eternal Peace
>
> No more with Reason & thyself at Strife;
> Give anxious Cares & endless Wishes room
> But thro' the cool sequester'd Vale of Life
> Pursue the silent Tenour of thy Doom.

The conclusion which the poet applies to his own case is presumably equally valid for the reader: it is foolish to repine because one is not a leading actor on the great stage of life.

The poem at this point clearly derives from a large family of moralizing poems written in the seventeenth and eighteenth centuries —a family that traced its ancestry back to the *Georgics* and to Horace, and included in its genealogical tree the Countess of Winchilsea's *Nocturnal Reverie* as well as Parnell's *Night-Piece on Death*. Tovey[9] considered that the original ending of the poem was bald and abrupt, although it may be doubted whether the average reader of the 1740's would have felt this: he would have recognised that he was reading a poem of a reassuringly familiar sort, in a metre that was just beginning to be fashionable.

Yet Gray himself was dissatisfied with the original ending. When

---

[9] *Gray's English Poems,* ed., D. C. Tovey (Cambridge, 1898), p. 153.

he sent the completed poem to Walpole he expressed the hope that he would "look upon it in the light of a *thing with an end to it; a* merit that most of my writings have wanted." [10] To bring this about he had not only worked hard: he had also made a radical change in the direction and meaning of the poem.

While both versions of the poem present us with Gray's Meditations among the Tombs, there are two great differences between the earlier version and that published in 1751. While it might be an overstatement to say simply that the later version is more "personal," it certainly tells us more about the poet. In the earlier version all that we hear of the poet is that he has been "with Reason & [himself] at Strife," troubled by "anxious Cares & endless Wishes." In the later version we hear how he would wander about or lie—like Jaques[11]—"And pore upon the brook that babbles by," so making himself ridiculous in the eyes of the country people who saw him. The first two stanzas of the Epitaph give us further information about him. Stylized as they are, the Poet himself has now become a part—and an important part—of the poem.[12] The second difference is that the original moral of the poem—that the poet (and presumably his readers) should be content to live in obscurity—is now dropped, in order to make way for a conclusion acknowledging his desire to be remembered after his death: a common human sentiment which he shares with the villagers buried in the churchyard. So a poem of Christian Stoicism is rewritten as a poem of Sensibility. The final statements made by the two versions of the poem are so different that it might be less misleading to regard the versions as two different poems.

We may conjecture that Gray's true reason for rejecting the earlier ending of the poem was not merely that it was too abrupt (Tovey's objection), but rather that it preached a Stoic attitude to life that he could not accept, at the deepest level of his mind and heart. Fortunately we can look over his shoulder and watch him arguing the point, in one of his Common Place Books. Under the heading "Affectus" [Passions] he records that "We find in A: Gellius, Lib: 19: Cap: 12: a discourse of Herodes Atticus, a Great Man of his time, where he argues against the Apathy of the Stoicks with much Good Sense." I quote in English the passage which Gray goes on to quote in Latin:

[10] *Correspondence*, I, 327.

[11] Mason refers to Gray's "moralizing Muse" in his "Elegy II: Written in a Church-Yard in South Wales, 1787," adding a note: "This Epithet is used to call to the Reader's recollection a passage in Shakespear, descriptive of a Character to which in its best parts Mr. Gray's was not dissimilar." The character is Jaques.

[12] It will be apparent that I disagree in many respects with Frank H. Ellis's most interesting essay, "Gray's *Elegy*: The Biographical Problem in Literary Criticism" [pp. 51ff.], and in particular with his view that "in his revision of the *Stanza's,* what Gray did was to depersonalize them entirely."

That no man, who felt and thought normally, could be wholly exempt and free from those emotions of the mind, which he called πάθη, caused by sorrow, desire, fear, anger and pleasure; and even if he could so resist them as to be free from them altogether, he would not be better off, since his mind would grow weak and sluggish, being deprived of the support of certain emotions, as of a highly necessary stimulus. . . . Those disciples of insensibility, wishing to be thought calm, courageous and steadfast because of showing neither desire nor grief, neither wrath nor joy, root out all the more vigorous emotions of the mind, and grow old in the torpor of a sluggish and, as it were, nerveless life.[13]

Gray comments that "The Passions, as Mr Lock has shew'd, are in the human Mind but Modes of Pleasure & of Pain, & consequently can never be eradicated, while it shall continue to covet Good, & to avoid Evil, that is in other Terms, as long as it exists; but they not only are in the Mind, it is necessary to our Wellbeing, that they should be there. We should be in the state almost of mere Vegetables without them, for why should we act, but to some End, & what end can we have, but to gain the pleasure resulting from some Good, or avoid the Pain accompanying, what we call Evil?" A few lines later we find Gray quoting from the Second Epistle of the *Essay on Man*. Although he does not here quote lines 101–2, it is clear that they were often in his mind:

> In lazy Apathy let Stoics boast
> Their Virtue fix'd; 'tis fix'd as in a frost.

In the passage about Grief and Compassion which makes up part of the entry "Affectus" we find (I think) the matrix of Gray's famous Latin stanza on the Tears of Sensibility. "Grief inclines, & softens us to commiserate, & redress, if we be able, the Misfortunes of others in the like unhappy Circumstances; indeed we should be insensible to their Woes,

> Non ignara mali, miseris succurrere disco,[14]

had we not felt, what it was to be wretched; nor could we form any Idea of them, but by comparison with our own:

> mollissima corda
> Humano generi dare se Natura fatetur,
> Quae lacrymas dedit. Haec nostri pars optima sensus:[15]

---

[13] Common Place Books, I, 3. Most of the passages from the Common Place Books which I quote have appeared in print before, but I take my text direct from the MS. For the translation of Aulus Gellius I rely on the Loeb edition of *The Attic Nights*, trans. John C. Rolfe, III (1952), 395–97.

[14] [Not unacquainted with misfortunes, I learn to help the wretched. . . . *Aeneid*, I, 630.]

[15] [Nature, who has given tears, acknowledges that she has given very tender hearts to the human race. This is the noblest part of our feeling. Juvenal, XV, 131–33.]

Compassion then, the Mother of so many generous actions, arises from this." It is an easy transition from these speculations to line 16 of the "Hymn to Adversity"—

> And from her own she learn'd to melt at others' woe

—or line 32:

> And Pity, dropping soft the sadly-pleasing tear.

The transition to the Alcaic stanza is no less clear:

> O lachrymarum Fons, tenero sacros
> Ducentium ortus ex animo; quater
>   Felix! in imo qui scatentem
>   Pectore te, pia Nympha, sensit! [16]

It seems to me that this same entry also throws light on Gray's acknowledgment of the human desire to be remembered after death: an acknowledgment which is so central to the concluding stanzas of the 1751 *Elegy*. Lines 85–88—

> For who to dumb Forgetfulness a prey,
> This pleasing anxious being e'er resign'd,
> Left the warm precincts of the chearful day,
> Nor cast one longing ling'ring look behind?

—might have been written as an explicit challenge to "the Apathy of the Stoicks." By ending the poem with a recognition of our unwillingness to be forgotten Gray is making it clear that he is not one of the "apathiae sectatores" who refuse to acknowledge human instincts and passions. Like the simple villagers, the poet himself participates in that species of self-love which makes us wish to be remembered and paid "the passing tribute of a sigh."

Such an apparent shift of sensibility as that between these two versions of Gray's poem, at the still centre of the eighteenth century, must arrest our attention. Only two years after the *Elegy* was published Rousseau was to write his *Discours Sur l'Origine et les Fondements de l'Inégalité parmi les hommes*, quoting the second of the Virgilian passages that we have just seen in Gray's Common Place Book in order to illustrate "le pur mouvement de la nature, antérieur à toute réflexion." [17] I do not wish to argue that Gray's own sensibility was transformed between the date of the earlier version of his poem and that of the later: that would be a naïve and melodramatic account

---

[16] [O fountain of tears which have their sacred sources in the sensitive soul! Four times blessed he who has felt thee, holy Nymph, bubbling up from the depths of his heart!]

[17] Ed., F. C. Green (Cambridge, 1941), p. 54.

of the matter. The interesting thing is that he was capable of writing both versions, at about the same point in his life, but felt that the later version was somehow truer to human nature, and therefore more satisfying. And so it came about that a poem which was already accepted as a classic soon after the middle of the eighteenth century continued to be regarded as a classic in the following century, when the Poet himself was so often to be the subject of the poem, and when topics from humble life were to call forth tears from a greater poet than Gray:

> To me the meanest flower that blows can give
> Thoughts that do often lie too deep for tears.

Yet we must not exaggerate. One has only to recall the poetry of the nineteenth century to acknowledge that the *Elegy* remains a highly formalized composition. We must bear this in mind when we consider Mason's suggestion that its composition was closely connected with the death of West.

It is true that West's friendship had meant a great deal to Gray. Walpole and West appealed to two facets of Gray's character, and it was West who appealed to the more important—the poet and the man of Sensibility. "I well remember how little you love Letters, where all the Materials are drawn out of oneself," Gray wrote to Walpole four years after West's death, while in another letter he remarks: "Of all people living I know you are the least a friend to letters spun out of one's own brains, with all the toil and constraint that accompanies sentimental productions." [18] The letters beween Gray and West, on the other hand, have all the features of a sentimental correspondence. On the 5th of June 1740, for example, we find West writing to Gray in the vein that we associate with the Man of Feeling thirty years later, and Gray replying that he has "not a thought, or even a weakness, I desire to conceal from you." In the same vein, West more than once expressed the hope that Gray would remember him after his death:

> Unknown & silent will depart my breath,
> Nor nature e'er take notice of my death.
> Yet some there are (ere sunk in endless night)
> Within whose breasts my monument I'd write. . . .[19]

On a later occasion Gray makes a similar request, with the characteristically Sentimental anticipation of his own death:

[18] *Correspondence*, I, 231, 326.
[19] I quote West's lines as they occur in Gray's Common Place Book, I, 105. As Toynbee and Whibley point out (III, 1199), the versions published by Mason seem to have been "corrected and improved."

> Then to my quiet Urn awhile draw near,
> And say, (while o'er the place you drop a Tear)
> Love & the Fair were of his Life the Pride,
> He lived, while She was kind, & when she frown'd, he died.
>
> (*Correspondence*, I, 199.)

The element of formality and convention in these passages is very obvious. West's poem is based on Tibullus III, v, and on a letter of Pope's to Steele, while Gray's lines are a translation of Propertius II, i. The earlier description of West as

> Of all our Youth th'Ambition & the Praise

no more corresponds to reality than does the statement that "Love & the Fair" were the "Pride" of Gray's life.

This perhaps makes it the less surprising that when we turn to the earlier of the extant versions of the *Elegy*, which must have been written closer to the date of West's death than the later, we find nothing that can be construed as an allusion to the death of Gray's friend. Several writers have pointed out that Gray echoes a phrase from one of West's poems in line 35.[20] But apart from that there is nothing in the first version of the poem to suggest West. Even in the second version one cannot do much more than echo the traditional conjecture that Gray may have had West in mind when he wrote the "Epitaph." That is not to suggest that the whole "Epitaph" is in fact about West: so far from being of "humble birth," he was—as Dodsley recorded in his *Collection of Poems*—"Son to the Chancellor of *Ireland,* and Grandson to Bishop BURNET." The line "He gave to Mis'ry all he had, a tear" may echo (as Tovey points out) a passage from Gray's tribute to the memory of West at the end of his *De Principiis Cogitandi*:

> has lachrymas, memori quas ictus amore
> Fundo; quod possum.[21]

Clearly the "Youth" of the "Epitaph" is a highly formalized figure, and the poet might well have devised a similar conclusion even if no close friend of his had in fact died. In any age friendship is an important part of the pattern of life, and it was as important to the eighteenth-century Man of Sensibility as it had been to the καλὸς κἀγαθός of Greek antiquity. The question of the identity of the "friend" in the "Epitaph" is a question of little critical significance—if indeed it is a meaningful question at all.

[20] "A Monody on the Death of Queen Caroline," in Dodsley's *Collection of Poems* (1748), II, 273. Cf. line 35 of the *Elegy*.

[21] [. . . these tears of mine, which, stricken as I am with love, I am shedding in memory of thee; I can do no more.]

This brings us back to the word "Elegy." When Mason remarked that "the subject authorized" Gray to call the poem an elegy, he did not necessarily mean that its subject was the death of a particular person. As Joseph Trapp had pointed out at the beginning of the century, "Elegies admit almost of any Matter, especially if it be treated of seriously. The Contempt of Riches, the Pleasures of the Country, are in great measure the Subject of them." [22] About the middle of the century the vogue for elegiac writing in this wide sense became very marked, and no one gives so helpful a description of "the *use* and *end* of elegy" as Shenstone:

> There is a truly virtuous pleasure connected with many pensive contemplations, which it is the province and excellency of elegy to enforce. This, by presenting suitable ideas, has discovered sweets in *melancholy* which we could not find in *mirth;* and has led us with success to the dusty *urn,* when we could draw no pleasure from the sparkling bowl; as pastoral conveys an idea of simplicity and innocence, it is in particular the task and merit of elegy to shew the innocence and simplicity of rural life to advantage; and that, in a way distinct from *pastoral,* as much as the plain but judicious landlord may be imagined to surpass his tenant both in *dignity* and *understanding.* It should also tend to elevate the more tranquil virtues of *humility, disinterestedness, simplicity,* and *innocence.*

Although Shenstone's "Prefatory Essay on Elegy" was not published until his *Works* were collected in 1764, two separate footnotes assure us that it had been written "near twenty years ago," so that his account of the matter dates from about the time when Gray was working on his *Elegy.* We know that Shenstone began writing his own *Elegies* in or about the year 1743, and it seems likely that Gray had seen at least two of them—IV and XV—before he wrote his own poem. Internal evidence based on echoes of Shenstone might, I think, be used to strengthen the case against the view that the *Elegy* was begun in 1742, but the argument would have to be extended to include other poems (such as the *Odes* of Collins and Joseph Warton) that Gray was reading in the later months of 1746. It is even conceivable that Gray saw a draft of Shenstone's "Prefatory Essay," and that this helped to define the tone of his own Elegy. But it is time to turn from conjecture to certainty, from the obscure history of its composition to the challenging fact of the poem itself.

While it seems likely that Gray's choice of stanza owed something to the example of Shenstone, he had already shown his liking for alternate rhyme in the "Sonnet on the Death of Richard West" (which has the rather unusual rhyme-scheme, abab, abab, cdcdcd), while his notes on Metre in his Common Place Books remind us that he was

---

[22] *Lectures on Poetry . . . Translated from the Latin* (1742), p. 165.

familiar with the cross-rhyming stanza in earlier English poetry. Under the heading, "The Measures I find principally in use among our Writers," we find the following:[23]

Verse	*Order of the Rhymes*
Stanza's, of four, as	Alternate. call'd by the French
L.ᵈ Surreys Verses, written in	Rime croisée, or entrelassée
Windsor-Castle. Epitaph on	(whether there were two, or more
Sʳ T: Wyat.&c:	Rhimes that answer'd one
Dryden's Annus Mirabilis.	another, as in all that we call
Spencer . . Colin-Clout's come	Stanza's
home again, & April. Gascoyne's	
Councell on travelling. his	
Woodmanship,	

Although it is unfortunate that this entry cannot be precisely dated, it matters less than it might because none of the examples that Gray mentions is of any importance as a model for the verse of his *Elegy*. It is in an earlier poem than *Annus Mirabilis,* the *Heroique Stanza's* to the memory of Cromwell, that we find Dryden coming closest to Gray's use of the metre. Gray must also have been familiar with Dryden's comment on the measure:

> I have chosen to write my Poem in *Quatrains* or *Stanza's* of four in alternate rhyme, because I have ever judg'd them more noble, and of greater dignity, both for the sound and number, than any other Verse in use amongst us.

Dryden goes on to acknowledge that he is making this high claim for quatrains in spite of the fact that he himself finds it easier to write in couplets,

> for there the work is sooner at an end, every two lines concluding the labour of the Poet: but in Quattrains he is to carry it farther on; and not onely so, but to bear along in his head the troublesome sense of four lines together. For those who write correctly in this kind must needs acknowledge, that the last line of the Stanza is to be consider'd in the composition of the first.

Annus Mirabilis may be taken to prove that quatrains are not a suitable metre for a long poem, but when Gray began his *Elegy* a recent poet was considered to have used the stanza successfully in the elegiac mode. Although Hammond's *Love Elegies* make insipid reading today, Gray is almost certain to have known them. In a letter Shenstone refers to the quatrain as "Hammond's Metre." [24] Here is his comment on the matter in his "Prefatory Essay":

[23] Common Place Books, II, 765. The poems of Gascoyne which Gray refers to may be found in *The Posies,* ed., John W. Cunliffe (Cambridge, 1907), pp. 344–52.
[24] *The Letters,* ed., Marjorie Williams (1939), p. 62.

The public ear, habituated of late to a quicker measure, may perhaps consider *this* as heavy and languid; but an objection of that kind may gradually lose its force, if this measure should be allowed to suit the nature of elegy.

The "quicker measure" was of course the pentameter couplet, as used by Pope; and there is no doubt that the slower movement of the quatrain is essential to the effect of Gray's *Elegy*. The best way to demonstrate this is to see what happens if we transpose two of its stanzas into couplets:

> The Curfew tolls the knell of parting day,
> The plowman homeward plods his weary way,
> The lowing herd wind slowly o'er the lea,
> And leaves the world to darkness and to me.
> . . . .
> Beneath those rugged elms, that yew-tree's shade,
> Each in his narrow cell for ever laid,
> Where heaves the turf in many a mould'ring heap,
> The rude Forefathers of the hamlet sleep.

It remains respectable verse; yet what has gone is the source of the peculiar distinction of the *Elegy*—the great suspended chords that sound through the poem and give it its characteristic inevitability.

The fact that so many of the stanzas of the *Elegy* can be transposed into couplets is a reminder that the greater part of the poem consists of more or less self-sufficient lines. Although Gray insisted that it should not be printed as separate quatrains, on only three occasions is the sense carried on from one quatrain to another. As a rule the first three lines lead with an air of finality to the fourth. Some of the most memorable lines—32, 56 and 76, for example—occur at the end of their quatrains. Gray understood as well as Dryden that "the last line of the stanza is to be considered in the composition of the first," and it was by remembering this that he was able to march so irresistibly towards the final assertion of line 36—

> The paths of glory lead but to the grave

or of line 92—

> Ev'n in our Ashes live their wonted Fires.

Such lines burst like great universal breakers on the shores of our limited personal experience.

The Common Place Books make it clear that the position of the caesura in a line of verse was one of the aspects of the Art of Poetry that interested Gray.[25] The use of the caesura most frequently noticed

[25] II, 757–59.

by modern critics of Augustan poetry is that which subserves the purposes of antithesis, as in Pope's line

Less wit than mimic, more a wit than wise.

In the *Elegy* Gray takes great care to avoid such antitheses. Most of the lines are without medial punctuation, and when such punctuation does occur, there is hardly ever the least hint of antithesis. On the contrary, the second half of the line is likely to amplify or parallel the first:

The boast of heraldry, the pomp of pow'r,
And all that beauty, all that wealth e'er gave.

Norton Nicholls tells us that the first line of the poem originally read

The curfew tolls the knell of *dying* day,

and that Gray changed "dying" to "parting" in order "to avoid the *concetto*." [26] This is easy to believe. Although I have argued that Gray did not, as he wrote the poem, think of himself as composing an "elegy" in the specialized sense, it is as true of him as of the writer of an elegy in Trapp's account of the genre that he "aims not to be witty or facetious, acrimonious or severe." Trapp rules that "with this Kind of Poem, every Thing that is epigrammatical, satirical, or sublime, is inconsistent." [27] Once or twice Gray does in fact approach the sublime, but throughout he carefully avoids the "epigrammatical [or] satirical." Gray had a flair for epigram, but "Nunc non erat his locus" [28] and throughout one notices that he avoids the kind of wit that makes a fleeting appearance in Pope's *Elegy to the Memory of an Unfortunate Lady*. He also avoids the temptation—always strong, for a poet writing in this metre—to use the last two lines for an image amplifying or illustrating the statement made in the first two—as Dryden so often does in *Annus Mirabilis*. The rhetoric of wit would be out of keeping with the spirit of the "autumnal Verses" in which Gray set down his reflections on human destiny.

From the first stanza onward we are aware that we are reading a carefully-patterned poem:

The *Curfew* tolls the knell | of parting *day*,
The lowing *herd* | winds slowly o'er the *lea*,

---

[26] *Correspondence*, III, 1, 297.
[27] *Lectures on Poetry*, p. 169.
[28] Horace's phrase, quoted by Dryden near the end of the preface to *Annus Mirabilis*.

The *plowman* homeward <u>plods</u> | his weary *way,*
And <u>leaves</u> the *world* | to *darkness* and to me.[29]

We notice at once that the movement of the first and third lines,
in which the caesura falls after the sixth syllable, differs from that
of the second and fourth, in which it falls after the fourth syllable.
We also notice that each line contains a substantive in each of its
halves, and that five of the eight half-lines also contain an adjective
or adverb. The lonely position of the words "and to me" at the end
of the quatrain gives them an effect of what might be termed pathetic
emphasis. When we move to the second quatrain we find Gray subtly
and skilfully gaining an effect of varied continuity:

Now <u>fades</u> the glimmering *landscape* | on the *sight,*
And all the *air* | a solemn *stillness* <u>holds,</u>
<u>Save</u> where the *beetle* | <u>wheels</u> his droning *flight,*
And drowsy *tinklings* | <u>lull</u> the distant *folds.*

Here the way in which the caesura in the first line falls after seven
syllables (or, more precisely, after seven and a half) differentiates it
sharply from any line in the preceding stanzas, as does the fact that
the initial verbs occur in the first foot of line 1 and the last foot of
line 2. Otherwise there is a general similarity of pattern. Once again
each line contains two nouns, one in each half: once again the noun
is usually preceded by an adjective or adverb. The last line quoted
may well remind us of Latin verse. In the preface to *Sylvae* Dryden
remarks that Claudian has only four or five types of line in his
repertoire,

perpetually closing his sence at the end of a Verse, and that Verse commonly which they call golden, or two Substantives and two Adjectives
with a Verb betwixt them to keep the peace.

The term "golden verse" or "golden line" is commonly used by classical
scholars to describe a line in which two adjectives are followed by
a verb and then two substantives. As Latin is an inflected language,
there is no doubt which adjective accompanies each substantive:

Mollia luteolâ <u>pingit</u> *vaccinia calthâ.*[30]

In view of the great popularity and influence of the *Georgics,* in
which such lines are relatively common, the question of the English

---

[29] I have tried to emphasize the pattern by italicizing nouns, underlining verbs,
and double-spacing adjectives, present participles and significant adverbs. I have
taken "tolls the knell" as a verbal phrase.

[30] Virgil, *Eclogues,* II, 50: "sets off the delicate hyacinth with the golden marigold."

equivalent of the "golden line" is a matter of some interest. The nearest equivalent would appear to be a line in which the principal words follow the sequence adjective-noun-verb-adjective-noun. The *Elegy* contains almost a dozen examples:

> Chill *Penury* repress'd their noble *rage*.

Such analysis further reveals that the commonest line-pattern of all in the *Elegy* follows the general sequence adjective-noun-adjective-noun, as in line 17:

> The breezy *call* of incense-breathing *Morn,*

or line 57:

> Some village-*Hampden,* that with dauntless *breast*.

There are fifteen or more lines of this general type, and we notice that they often occur first in their quatrains. There is a different type of line which tends to occur fourth in its quatrain, and on occasion in the third and fourth lines successively. This consists of verb-noun-adjective-noun (sometimes with an adjective before the first noun, and sometimes with another verb at the end):

> To scatter *plenty* o'er a smiling *land,*
> And read their *hist'ry* in a nation's *eyes*.

It is not suggested that the essence of the *Elegy* is to be found in any formula. Yet it is (after all) the poem *par excellence* of recurrent patterns and subtle variations from the established norm, and to discern the shadow of the "golden line" and of what may be termed the balanced adjectival line beneath the surface of the verse may help us to appreciate the rhetorical structure of this remarkable composition.

As we study the diction of the *Elegy* we are supported by the knowledge that Gray himself had decided views on the nature of the language that a poet should use. His most celebrated observation occurs in a letter to West. In April, 1742 Gray had sent him a long speech from a projected tragedy, *Agrippina,* and West had replied that he considered the style "too antiquated," recommending the example of Racine, who "no where gives you the phrases of Ronsard: His language is the language of the times." Gray replied:

> As to matter of stile, I have this to say: The language of the age is never the language of poetry; except among the French, whose verse, where the thought or image does not support it, differs in nothing from prose. Our poetry, on the contrary, has a language peculiar to itself; to which almost every one, that has written, has added something by enriching it with foreign idioms and derivatives. (*Correspondence,* I, 189–92.)

West proceeded, very sensibly, to limit the range of disagreement
by reminding Gray of the criterion of appropriateness:

> Old words revived . . . [are] of excellent use in *tales*. . . . One need
> only read Milton to acknowledge the dignity they give *the Epic*. . . .
> They ought to be used in *Tragedy* more sparingly, than in most *kinds* of
> poetry. (I, 195; my italics.)

"A Long Story" exemplifies the sort of "language" that Gray considered appropriate to light verse:

> Each hole and cupboard they explore,
> Each creek and cranny of his chamber,
> Run hurry-skurry round the floor,
> And o'er the bed and tester clamber.

What we are concerned with in the *Elegy* is the "language" proper
to one sort of poetry: a species of meditative poetry written in an
elegiac mood.

Once or twice the language of the poem comes close to that of
"the age," as in lines 3–4; but they are quite exceptional. It is true
that when we analyse the diction we find no words of Gray's own
"invention" and none even of his own "composition" (unless "ivy-
mantled" or "incense-breathing" is new, which seems unlikely). Such
an analysis reveals that a considerable number of the words in the
poem are slightly archaic and poetical—words like jocund, oft, yonder,
bower, glebe and save (= except). We also notice that most of the
nouns and verbs are everyday words, usually monosyllabic; and that
there is a remarkably high number of adjectives. But the most important result of the analysis is to remind us that "language" consists
of *words as they are used* and not as separate and independent enti-
ties. Wordsworth's failure to understand this is one of the sources
of the confusion in the Preface to the second edition of *Lyrical Ballads*.
As soon as we look at the *Elegy* again with this in mind we find that
its "language" is very remote from that of "the age":

> The struggling pangs of conscious truth to hide,
> To quench the blushes of ingenuous shame,
> Or heap the shrine of Luxury and Pride
> With incense kindled at the Muse's flame.

There is hardly a word there which Gray might not have used in
conversation, but the way in which the words are being made to
work is not the prose way. In the space that remains I wish to examine one or two aspects of the "peculiar language" of our poetry
as exemplified in this poem.

Every reader notices Gray's use of abstract personifications, which is reminiscent of *The Vanity of Human Wishes*. Like Johnson, Gray uses personification in a non-pictorial way natural to a scholar conversant in Latin poetry. It is perfectly true that the presence or absence of a capital letter may be all that determines our decision whether or not a given abstraction is a personification. There seems no particular reason why "Luxury" and "Pride" should be capitalized, in line 71, while "conscious truth" and "ingenuous shame" in lines 69–70 are not. In fact, it hardly matters. Like Johnson, Gray has no wish to "bring his personifications to life": like Johnson, he is using them to gain weight and conciseness, as in lines 49–50:

> But Knowledge to their eyes her ample page
> Rich with the spoils of time did ne'er unroll.

Gray was worried by what he regarded as the increasing flabbiness of the English language. His use of abstract personifications was a device to escape from the wordiness of English, and the "concise sententiousness" for which he elsewhere praises Tacitus is equally characteristic of the stanza in which he himself makes the transition from his initial description of the villagers to the weighty reflections which follow:

> Let not Ambition mock their useful toil,
> Their homely joys, and destiny obscure;
> Nor Grandeur hear with a disdainful smile,
> The short and simple annals of the poor.

Such a grave sententiousness follows naturally from the highly generalized observations which have gone before:

> The breezy call of incense-breathing Morn,
> The swallow twitt'ring from the straw-built shed,
> The cock's shrill clarion, or the echoing horn,
> No more shall rouse them from their lowly bed.

Here we are in the generalized world of "L'Allegro" and "Il Penseroso," and it might be said of the *Elegy* as truly as it was of Milton's poems that "it is not a particular ploughman, milkmaid, and shepherd that [Gray] sees." To explain this lack of particularity T. S. Eliot invoked Milton's later blindness, his love of music, his limited sensuousness and "the peculiar education which he received." [31] Now Gray was not blind, and while the education that he received must have resembled Milton's in most respects—although it was less abnormally intense—his meticulous notes and his exquisite little drawings of birds and insects remain as evidence that his sensory perceptions were

[31] "A Note on the Verse of John Milton," *Essays and Studies by Members of the English Association*, xxi, 1936.

in no way impaired. If his descriptions are generalized, it is because
he wishes them to be generalized: because particularity would ruin
the effect that he is bent on achieving.

Another striking feature of the language of the *Elegy* is the fre-
quency with which Gray uses verbs or verbal phrases which would
not occur in prose and which strike the reader as slightly foreign
even in verse. Like the abstract personifications, these are almost
entirely confined to the part of the poem which is already present
in the earlier version. I have in mind such phrases as "the air . . . a
. . . stillness holds," "wheels his . . . flight," "ply her . . . care,"
"oft did the harvest to their sickle yield," and "how bow'd the woods
beneath their . . . stroke." It is at once obvious that a number of
these and other similar locutions are of Latin origin. In "repress'd
their noble rage," for example, the word "rage" is an English equivalent of the word "furor," with the favorable meaning that it bears
in such a phrase as "furor poeticus"; while the verbal usage may be
paralleled by such a phrase as "furorem exsultantem reprimere" in
Cicero (*Pro Sestio,* 44, 95). It is unnecessary to search for particular
instances of Latin parallels to "impute the fault" and "provoke the
dust." "Ply her care" is obviously an instance of "cura," one of
Virgil's favorite words, influencing the English idiom. Latin parallels
for most of the other locutions of this sort could readily be found. It
is no surprise that the *Elegy* should have been translated into Latin
more often and more successfully (perhaps) than any other English
poem.

It is not suggested that no one had used these phrases in English
before. On the contrary, a careful search through the pages of Milton,
Cowley, Dryden, Pope and Thomson would no doubt produce parallels for every idiom of this sort, while many might be traced further
back to Spenser, Shakespeare and the Elizabethan translators.

But that is not the point. Gray liked these expressions precisely
because they are Latinate. As he was in the habit of reading and
writing Latin more or less daily throughout his life, he must sometimes
have used a Latin idiom without caring whether it had been used by an
earlier English writer or not. When he knew that it had, he no doubt
regarded it as one of the "foreign idioms and derivatives" with which
his predecessors had enriched the language of English poetry. He found
that such phrases enabled him to achieve effects which he could not
achieve in any other way.

Gray knew what to take from Latin: he also knew what to avoid. We
have only to look into Thomson to find the sort of empty Latinate poly-
syllables which are notably absent from the *Elegy*:

> Now, by the cool declining year condensed,
> Descend the copious exhalations.   (*Autumn,* 707–8.)

In the same way, Gray avoids tired classical mythology: his owl complains to "the Moon," not to Cynthia, while the *Elegy* contains no parallel to the line

> And redning Phoebus lifts his golden Fire

in the earlier *Sonnet on the Death of Richard West*. Gray banishes "fleecy care" and "finny tribe," and with them the whole outdated charade of the pastoral convention; while in the revised text of the poem Cato, Tully and Caesar make way for Hampden, Milton and Cromwell. This does not mean that Gray wished to write directly about country people—he was no Crabbe, still less a Clare. His subject is Man, and he does not affect familiarity with the inhabitants of the village. His idiom keeps them at the distance appropriate to the sort of picture that he intends to paint.

The same generalizing effect may be noticed in Gray's use of adjectives and present participles. They are so numerous that many critics have agreed with Goldsmith that the *Elegy* is "overloaded with epithet." Every other noun is accompanied by an adjective, and as most of the nouns are monosyllabic and most of the adjectives are not, it becomes apparent how important a part the adjectives play in the final texture of the verse. Goldsmith pointed out that parts of the poem may be reduced to tetrameters by the simple expedient of omitting some of the adjectives:

> The Curfew tolls the knell of day,
> The herd wind slowly o'er the lea,
> The plowman homeward plods his way. . . .[32]

—an experiment which reminds us once again that the *Elegy* stands in the line of descent from "Il Penseroso." Often a noun is accompanied by a composite adjective, or by two separate adjectives—as in "dark unfathom'd caves" and "cool sequester'd vale." In lines 85–88 only one of the six nouns is without an adjective, and two of them have two adjectives each:

> For who to dumb Forgetfulness a prey,
> This pleasing anxious being e'er resign'd,
> Left the warm precincts of the chearful day,
> Nor cast one longing ling'ring look behind?

The same stanza may serve as a reminder of the importance of present participles, which is particularly marked in the opening stanzas. Throughout there is something ambivalent about their effect. On the one hand they give the lines a static, pictorial quality: on the other they

---

[32] *Boswell's Life of Johnson*, ed., G. Birkbeck Hill, Rev. L. F. Powell, I, 404n. In the second line Goldsmith omitted "slowly," not "lowing."

draw our attention insistently to the impermanence of the scene which we are regarding—the impermanence of every human scene. Jean Hagstrum has pointed out that Gray seems to have been remembering Poussin's great painting, "The Shepherds of Arcady," as he wrote the concluding lines.[33] There is a profound nostalgia in these lines, the nostalgia of Virgil's "lacrimae rerum," the nostalgia of mankind aware of mortality. That nostalgia is the subject of the poem.

[33] Jean Hagstrum, *The Sister Arts* (Chicago, 1958), 292–301.

PART FOUR

View Points

William Empson: Proletarian Literature

Gray's *Elegy* is an odd case of poetry with latent political ideas:

> Full many a gem of purest ray serene
> The dark, unfathomed caves of ocean bear;
> Full many a flower is born to blush unseen
> And waste its sweetness on the desert air.

What this means, as the context makes clear, is that eighteenth-century England had no scholarship system or *carrière ouverte aux talents*. This is stated as pathetic, but the reader is put into a mood in which one would not try to alter it. (It is true that Gray's society, unlike a possible machine society, was necessarily based on manual labor, but it might have used a man of special ability wherever he was born.) By comparing the social arrangement to Nature he makes it seem inevitable, which it was not, and gives it a dignity which was undeserved. Furthermore, a gem does not mind being in a cave and a flower prefers not to be picked; we feel that the man is like the flower, as short-lived, natural, and valuable, and this tricks us into feeling that he is better off without opportunities. The sexual suggestion of *blush* brings in the Christian idea that virginity is good in itself, and so that any renunciation is good; this may trick us into feeling it is lucky for the poor man that society keeps him unspotted from the World. The tone of melancholy claims that the poet understands the considerations opposed to aristocracy, though he judges against them; the truism of the reflections in the churchyard, the universality and impersonality this gives to the style, claim as if by comparison that we ought to accept the injustice of society as we do the inevitability of death.

Many people, without being communists, have been irritated by the complacence in the massive calm of the poem, and this seems partly because they feel there is a cheat in the implied politics; the "bourgeois" themselves do not like literature to have too much "bourgeois ideology."

And yet what is said is one of the permanent truths; it is only in degree that any improvement of society could prevent wastage of human powers; the waste even in a fortunate life, the isolation even of a life rich in intimacy, cannot but be felt deeply, and is the central feeling of tragedy. And anything of value must accept this because it must not prostitute itself; its strength is to be prepared to waste itself, if it does not get its opportunity. A statement of this is certainly non-political because it is true in any society, and yet nearly all the great poetic statements of it are in a way "bourgeois," like this one; they suggest to many readers, though they do not say, that for the poor man things cannot be improved even in degree. This at least shows that the distinction the communists try to draw is a puzzling one; two people may get very different experiences from the same work of art without either being definitely wrong. One is told that the Russians now disapprove of tragedy, and that there was a performance of *Hamlet* in the Turk-Sib region which the audience decided spontaneously was a farce. They may well hold out against the melancholy of old Russia, and for them there may be dangerous implications in any tragedy, which other people do not see. I am sure at any rate that one could not estimate the amount of bourgeois ideology "really in" the verse from Gray.

Carl J. Weber: The Bicentenary of Gray's "Elegy"

[Shepard and Wood in their *English Prose and Poetry 1660–1800*, p. 519, remark that "the *Elegy* is a noble phrasing of commonplace thought . . . gathered from the literature of the world. . . . It is a triumph of patient art rather than of genius."]

Is it not curious that in all this chorus of praise on both sides of the Atlantic, we fail to hear any voice raised in praise of the real mark of Gray's originality, the real reason for his being taken to the heart of the world?

Oh to love so, be so loved, yet so mistaken!

Not that the critics are mistaken in calling our attention to Gray's fine ear, to his excellent choice of adjectives, to the accuracy of his descriptions of nature, to his divine truisms, to the music of his "measure," to his felicity in the creation of phrases that hook themselves into our memory: all this is true enough. But it is not the whole truth.

The truly original note in the *Elegy* was identified by President

"The Bicentenary of Gray's 'Elegy,'" by *Carl J. Weber.* From the Colby Library Quarterly, *Series III, No. 1 (February, 1951), 9–12. Copyright © 1951 by* Colby Library Quarterly. *Reprinted by permission of the editor.*

Arthur J. Roberts of Colby College on Sunday, June 27, 1920, in the
course of a baccalaureate sermon which he preached to the graduating
class. Said President Roberts:

> Gray's *Elegy*, the richest bequest of eighteenth century English litera-
> ture, has for its central theme the idea of undeveloped human power.
>
> > Perhaps in this neglected spot is laid
> > Some heart once pregnant with celestial fire;
> > Hands that the rod of empire might have swayed
> > Or waked to ecstasy the living lyre.
>
> That is, perhaps in this graveyard lies some man who, under other and
> favoring circumstances, might have been a great statesman or a great poet,
> but who lived out his life . . . without giving evidence . . . of the pos-
> session of extraordinary powers.

In these words of Arthur J. Roberts (Colby, '90), the "central theme"
of Gray's *Elegy* is given the emphasis it deserves. Thomas Gray
wrote his poem about the "rude forefathers of the hamlet" two
hundred years ago. Let the date sink in. Then ask yourself: Who,
before Gray, had celebrated the "homely joys and destiny obscure"
of the ordinary man? Where in Shakespeare or Milton or Dryden or
Pope can you read "the short and simple annals of the poor"? In
Shakespeare, poor men are "the common herd" or "the tag-rag people," or mere "varletry," or "the rabblement," and Shakespeare's
successors learned well the snobbish lesson he had taught them, that
whereas

> The heavens themselves blaze forth the death of princes,
> When beggars die there are no comets seen.

Gray's unprecedented and courageous act lay in his addressing his
elegy to the memory, not of "princes," but of humble workmen,
buried in now-neglected graves after living lives of hard-handed toil.

Gray's critics can be so smugly superior in their verdict that the
Elegy "is not the most original in our language" and that it has
charmed all ears but "not through any originality of thought"; but
where is their recognition of the true originality of Gray's democratic
sympathy? Gray wrote twenty-five years before the American Revolution; he wrote forty years before the French Revolution. Goldsmith's *Deserted Village,* with its celebration of "a bold peasantry,
their country's pride," follows the *Elegy* by almost twenty years.
Burns's "A man's a man for a' that" is a quarter of a century later
still. If Gray's solicitous interest in the dwellers in "this neglected
spot" isn't original and new—and very modern—let the critics an-
nounce the source from which he borrowed the idea. Thomas Gray is
the pioneer literary spokesman for the Ordinary Man, the patron

saint of the Unknown Soldier; and the year 1751, in which Gray put
his finger on ignorance and "chill penury" as the two greatest foes
of the common man, is the literary landmark from which we can date
and measure modern literature with far greater justice than we exhibit
when we date it all from 1798, the year in which Wordsworth published his *Lyrical Ballads*. Gray's "rude forefathers of the hamlet"
were also the forefathers of Wordsworth's Wagoner, and of his
Michael, and of his Peter Bell.

Joseph Foladare: Gray's "Frail Memorial" to West

[Foladare discusses how serious a loss West's death was to Gray,
Gray's English sonnet and Latin verse on the death of West, and the
influence of Milton on Gray. He mentions Shepard's "positive identification" of West as the "Youth" in the "Epitaph."]

The critics and scholars must be both right and wrong. The tone
of sorrow which informs much of the *Elegy* can be ascribed to the loss
of West, whether the poem is considered to have been started in 1742
or a few years later. In February 1747—some three years before he
completed the *Elegy*—Gray listed the poems by West in his possession,
in preparation for a volume of his and West's collected works. To
Walpole, who had proposed the venture, he wrote: "I should not
care, how unwise the ordinary Sort of Readers might think my
Affection for him provided those few, that ever loved any Body, or
judged of any thing rightly, might from such little Remains be moved
to consider, what he would have been; and to wish, that Heaven had
granted him a longer Life, and a Mind more at Ease" (*Corres.*, p. 266).
The intensity of his feelings did not diminish. Over twenty years later,
whenever his recently-found friend Norton Nicholls "mentioned Mr.
West he looked serious, and seemed to feel the affliction of a recent
loss" (*Corres.*, p. 1300). At the same time it is clear that during the
period of composition of the *Elegy* Gray was forced to think again
about his own career, to reflect on the meaning of fame and on the
quality of true and admirable achievement.[1] He too was still to
make his mark. In the above-mentioned letter to Walpole he said
of his and West's poems, "I must fear our Joynt-Stock would hardly
compose a small Volume." But attempts to make either West or
Gray the subject of the *Elegy* invariably pauperize the poem and reflect

---

"Gray's 'Frail Memorial' to West," by Joseph Foladare. From PMLA, *LXXV
(1960), 61–65. Copyright © 1960 by the Modern Language Association of America.
Reprinted by permission of the MLA.*

[1] See Ellis, pp. 51ff.

profoundly on the author's artistic intelligence. My effort now will be strictly to show that Gray's problem of personal loss, first expressed in the sonnet and in the Latin lines, is finally resolved in the *Elegy*.

In the four quatrains which Johnson noted as "original" the poem moves from a description of the "rude Forefathers of the hamlet" and their unrealized potentials, and the assertion that absence of worldly achievement was in their lives balanced by other virtues, to the universal desire for a memorial, material, even personal:

> Yet ev'n these bones from insult to protect
> Some frail memorial still erected nigh. . . .
>
> For who to dumb Forgetfulness a prey,
> This pleasing anxious being e'er resign'd,
> Left the warm precincts of the chearful day,
> Nor cast one longing ling'ring look behind?
>
> On some fond breast the parting soul relies,
> Some pious drops the closing eye requires;
> Ev'n from the tomb the voice of Nature cries,
> Ev'n in our Ashes live their wonted Fires.[2]

Gray's Latin tribute to West had ended: "look then upon these tears of mine; while I indulge my grief (what can I more?) beside your tomb, and scatter these vain offerings on your unanswering ashes" (Ketton-Cremer's trans.). Are there also echoes from the sonnet in "the warm precincts of the chearful day"? And could Gray, who in 1747 had prepared for publication the following lines by West,[3] have been moved by them?

> Few will lament my loss whene'er I die. . . .
> Unknown and silent will depart my breath,
> Nor Nature e'er take notice of my death.
> Yet some there are (ere spent my vital days)
> Within whose breasts my tomb I wish to raise.

The unhonored dead of the churchyard found their poet, who is described to the narrator by the "hoary-headed Swain." But Gray too could wish to be such a poet and supply "the place of fame and elegy" for West. Now, whether one finds in the poem, with Ellis,[4] dramatis personae consisting of (1) the semi-literate Stonecutter, (2) the Spokesman and author of the epitaph-writer's epitaph ("me" of line 4), (3)

---

[2] The last line, as Johnson must have known from Mason's edition, is an "imitation" from Petrarch, Sonnet 169. Ellis (p. 67, n. 17) also notes a parallel to Propertius.

[3] See Leonard Whibley, *Corres.*, Appendix C, "Gray's Corrections of West's Poems," pp. 1199–1200.

[4] See n. 1.

the peasant narrator ("hoary-headed Swain"), and (4) enquiring wayfarer ("kindred Spirit")—and consequently sees "The Epitaph" as
applying to the Stonecutter, or whether one simply considers the "me"
(line 4), "thee" (line 93), and "thou" (line 115) as applying through
successsive shifts in perspective and time to the "author" of the poem
and the subject of "The Epitaph," he must sense that the poet who
often was seen "at the peep of dawn/Brushing with hasty steps the
dews away/To meet the sun upon the upland lawn" bears a kinship
to West and Gray. Shepard (p. 371) indeed finds in the first seven lines
of the description exact parallels to portions of a poem West had
sent to Gray. But both West and Gray were fond of describing themselves as traditional pastoral poets, as in Gray's "Barbares Aedes"
and "Mater Rosarum" and in his well-known letter to Walpole
(*Corres.*, pp. 47–48, 85–86, 158–159). In the lines on the village poet
Gray and West once again join the company of Vergil and Milton, as
they did in the sonnet. And in claiming membership in an immortal
band, of poets famous and now a poet "to Fame unknown," Gray
finds for West and even for himself more than "the passing tribute
of a sigh." The memorial to West is complete; and Gray can go "To-
morrow to fresh woods, and pastures new."

Chronology of Important Dates

	Gray	The Age
1716	Dec. 26: Thomas Gray born.	
1721–42		Political dominance of Sir Robert Walpole.
1725–34	At Eton.	
1726		Swift's *Gulliver's Travels*. Thomson's *Seasons* (1726–30).
1728		Pope's *Dunciad*.
1731–38		Pope's *Epistles* and *Imitations of Horace*.
1734	July 4: Entered Peterhouse College.	
1735–38	Cambridge and London.	
1739–41	Grand Tour of France, Switzerland, and Italy with Horace Walpole.	
1740		War of the Austrian Succession begins.
1741	Sept.: Returned to London.	
1742	June: *Ode on the Spring* and death of West. Aug.: *Sonnet on the Death of West, Ode on a Distant Prospect of Eton College, Ode (Hymn) to Adversity.*	
1742–45		Pope's *New Dunciad* (1742) and *Dunciad* (1743) in four books. Young's *Night Thoughts* (1742–45).

1743	Dec.: Took degree of Bachelor of Laws.	
1744		Death of Pope.
1745	Reconciliation with Walpole.	Stuart Rebellion of Bonnie Prince Charlie.
1746		Trial of the rebel peers. Collins' *Odes*.
1750	June: *Elegy* sent to Walpole.	
1751	Feb. 15: *Elegy* published.	
1752–57	*Bard* and *Progress of Poesy* written.	
1756–63		Seven Years War.
1757	Aug. 8: *Odes* published.	
1760		Death of George II. Macpherson's "translations" of Ossian.
1765		Percy's *Reliques* (ballads).
c. 1765– 70		Chatterton's poems.
1768	Mar. 12: *Poems* published. July 28: Appointed Regius Professor of Modern History at Cambridge.	
1771	July 30: Died.	

Notes on the Contributors

CLEANTH BROOKS, a former Rhodes Scholar, teaches at Yale and is particularly interested in the reading and interpreting of poetry; he is one of the best known of the "New Critics." His publications include *Modern Poetry and the Tradition, The Well Wrought Urn,* and *Modern Rhetoric.*

A. E. DYSON taught at the University College of North Wales and at the University of East Anglia, has written many critical essays on seventeenth- to twentieth-century literature, and is the author of *The Crazy Fabric: Essays in Irony* and the co-author of *Modern Poetry: Studies in Practical Criticism.*

FRANK HALE ELLIS taught at Yale and is now at Smith College. Among his publications in seventeenth- and eighteenth-century literature are "Gray's *Elegy:* the Biographical Problem in Literary Criticism" and "John Freke and *The History of Insipids.*"

WILLIAM EMPSON studied at Cambridge, has taught in the Far East, and is now at Sheffield University. His published poetry includes *Milton's God, Seven Types of Ambiguity, Some Versions of Pastoral,* and *Structure of Complex Words.* He is interested in the social significance of literature.

JOSEPH FOLADARE, now at the University of California, Santa Barbara, has been largely concerned with the eighteenth century. He is co-author of *Index to the Private Papers of James Boswell.*

LYLE GLAZIER studied at Harvard, is now at the State University of New York at Buffalo and is interested in English philology and Spenser. Two of his publications are "The Struggle between Good and Evil in the First Book of the *Faerie Queene*" and "The Nature of Spenser's Imagery."

IAN JACK is Lecturer in English at Cambridge University and Fellow of Pembroke College, which houses the most valuable of the Gray manuscripts. He has written *Augustan Satire, Pope,* and *Sir Walter Scott.*

W. M. NEWMAN was the first to point out the influence of the trial of the rebel peers on Gray's *Elegy.*

MORSE PECKHAM teaches at the University of South Carolina and has been interested in Victorian literature and its connections with the arts. He has edited Darwin's *Origin of the Species,* is author of *Beyond the Tragic Vision,* and co-author of *Word, Meaning, Poem.*

HERBERT W. STARR taught at Temple University, has published *Thomas Gray as a Literary Critic, A Bibliography of Thomas Gray,* and is the co-editor of the Clarendon edition of Gray's *Poems.*

JOHN HALE SUTHERLAND teaches at Colby College and has worked in eighteenth-century literature. His publications include studies of Blake and Swift and *Mr. Spectator's London.*

CARL J. WEBER, a former Guggenheim Fellow, was Professor Emeritus at Colby College and former editor of the *Colby Library Quarterly.* He published frequently in nineteenth-century literature and is the author of *Hardy of Wessex* and *Dearest Emmie.*

Selected Bibliography

(See also the publications noted in the Introduction.)

Bibliographies

Northup, Clark S., *A Bibliography of Thomas Gray* [through 1916], Cornell Studies in English, I. New Haven: Yale University Press, 1917.

Starr, Herbert W., *A Bibliography of Thomas Gray, 1917–1951* . . . , Temple University Publications. Philadelphia: University of Pennsylvania Press, 1953.

The Poetry

Fukuhara, Rintaro, and Henry Bergen, eds., *An Elegy Written in a Country Churchyard* . . . Primrose Hill, London: Walters and Miller, 1933.

Stokes, Francis G., ed., *An Elegy Written in a Country Churchyard* . . . Oxford: The Clarendon Press, 1929. The two above editions give detailed descriptions of the manuscripts and the variants in the early editions, including misprints.

Starr, H[erbert]. W., and J[ohn]. R. Hendrickson, eds., *The Complete Poems of Thomas Gray, English, Latin and Greek*. Oxford: The Clarendon Press 1966. Textual and explanatory notes, English translations of the Latin and Greek poems.

The Letters

Toynbee, Paget, and Leonard Whibley, eds., *The Correspondence of Thomas Gray*. Oxford: The Clarendon Press, 1935, 3v. Invaluable. Not only the best edition of the letters but an encyclopedia of information on almost any subject connected with Gray.

Critical Works

Golden, Morris, *Thomas Gray*. New York: Twayne's English Authors, 1964. Useful general study of Gray as a poet. Chapter on *Elegy* with discussion of recent criticism.

Jones, William Powell, *Thomas Gray, Scholar* . . . Cambridge: Harvard University Press, 1937. Excellent. Very reliable. The best and most thorough account of Gray's interests.

Ketton-Cremer, Robert W., *Thomas Gray: A Biography*. Cambridge, Eng.: Cambridge University Press, 1955. Based partly on earlier work done by the late Leonard Whibley. With the exception of the somewhat doubtful chapter (XII) on Bonstetten, by far the most detailed and reliable biography. Not to be confused with the author's much shorter 1935 biography of the same title.

Martin, Roger, *Essai sur Thomas Gray*. Paris: Les Presses Universitaires de France, 1934. In French. Very valuable. The most detailed study of Gray in print, but the "psychoanalytic" approach may not always be supported by evidence. Good critical discussion of the *Elegy*, pp. 424–36.